ESSENTIALS OF

Critical Participatory
Action Research

Essentials of Qualitative Methods Series

ESSENTIALS OF

Critical Participatory Action Research

Michelle Fine
María Elena Torre

 AMERICAN PSYCHOLOGICAL ASSOCIATION

Published by
American Psychological Association
750 First Street, NE
Washington, DC 20002
https://www.apa.org

Order Department
https://www.apa.org/pubs/books
order@apa.org

In the U.K., Europe, Africa, and the Middle East, copies may be ordered from Eurospan
https://www.eurospanbookstore.com/apa
info@eurospangroup.com

Typeset in Charter and Interstate by Circle Graphics, Inc., Reisterstown, MD

Printer: Gasch Printing, Odenton, MD
Cover Designer: Anne C. Kerns, Anne Likes Red, Inc., Silver Spring, MD

Library of Congress Cataloging-in-Publication Data

Names: Fine, Michelle, author. | Torre, María Elena, author.
Title: Essentials of critical participatory action research /
  by Michelle Fine and María Elena Torre.
Description: Washington, DC : American Psychological Association, [2021] |
Series: Essentials of qualitative methods series | Includes bibliographical references
  and index.
Identifiers: LCCN 2020054990 (print) | LCCN 2020054991 (ebook) |
  ISBN 9781433834615 (paperback) | ISBN 9781433837432 (ebook)
Subjects: LCSH: Action research—Methodology. | Participant observation.
Classification: LCC H62 .F434 2021 (print) | LCC H62 (ebook) | DDC 001.4—dc23
LC record available at https://lccn.loc.gov/2020054990
LC ebook record available at https://lccn.loc.gov/2020054991

https://doi.org/10.1037/0000241-000

Printed in the United States of America

10 9 8 7 6 5 4 3

This book is dedicated to everyone who has joined arms with us,
as researchers, colleagues, and friends, who share the belief that
social science has an important role to play in our struggles for justice.
May we never stop working, imagining, creating, and dancing for
a world where each and every one of us has all that we need
to breathe, dream, and flourish.

Contents

Series Foreword

Qualitative approaches have become accepted and indeed embraced as empirical methods within the social sciences, as scholars have realized that many of the phenomena in which we are interested are complex and require deep inner reflection and equally penetrating examination. Quantitative approaches often cannot capture such phenomena well through their standard methods (e.g., self-report measures), so qualitative designs using interviews and other in-depth data-gathering procedures offer exciting, nimble, and useful research approaches.

Indeed, the number and variety of qualitative approaches that have been developed is remarkable. We remember Bill Stiles saying (quoting Chairman Mao) at one meeting about methods, "Let a hundred flowers bloom," indicating that there are many appropriate methods for addressing research questions. In this series, we celebrate this diversity (hence, the cover design of flowers).

The question for many of us, though, has been how to decide among approaches and how to learn the different methods. Many prior descriptions of the various qualitative methods have not provided clear enough descriptions of the methods, making it difficult for novice researchers to learn how to use them. Thus, those interested in learning about and pursuing qualitative research need crisp and thorough descriptions of these approaches, with lots of examples to illustrate the method so that readers can grasp how to use the methods.

The purpose of this series of books, then, is to present a range of qualitative approaches that seemed most exciting and illustrative of the range of methods appropriate for social science research. We asked leading experts in qualitative methods to contribute to the series, and we were delighted that they accepted our invitation. Through this series, readers have the opportunity to learn qualitative research methods from those who developed the methods and/or who have been using them successfully for years.

We asked the authors of each book to provide context for the method, including a rationale, situating the method within the qualitative tradition, describing the method's philosophical and epistemological background, and noting the key features of the method. We then asked them to describe in detail the steps of the method, including the research team, sampling, biases and expectations, data collection, data analysis, and variations on the method. We also asked authors to provide tips for the research process and for writing a manuscript emerging from a study that used the method. Finally, we asked authors to reflect on the methodological integrity of the approach, along with the benefits and limitations of the particular method.

This series of books can be used in several different ways. Instructors teaching courses in qualitative research could use the whole series, presenting one method at a time to expose students to a range of qualitative methods. Alternatively, instructors could choose to focus on just a few approaches, as depicted in specific books, supplementing the books with examples from studies that have been published using the approaches, and providing experiential exercises to help students get started using the approaches.

This book describes critical participatory action research (CPAR), a method that fosters engagement between researchers and communities that seek to document, challenge, and transform conditions of social justice. Michelle Fine and María Elena Torre have upheld the mantra of "No research on us, without us" throughout their more than 25 years of research experience with a range of communities (e.g., prisoners, students, domestic violence survivors, asylum seekers) facing multiple injustices. The powerful examples they include here will stimulate readers to deeply examine the foundational questions and processes inherent in engaging in research with communities.

—*Clara E. Hill and Sarah Knox*

ESSENTIALS OF
Critical Participatory
Action Research

1

CRITICAL PARTICIPATORY ACTION RESEARCH

Conceptual Foundations

Critical participatory action research (CPAR) is a framework for engaging research with communities interested in documenting, challenging, and transforming conditions of social injustice. The preposition "with" matters enormously. It marks a dramatic shift in the design of research as usual, breaking from conventional approaches in which academics research and write "about" or "on" communities as objects of study. CPAR, instead, asserts all people's right to research (Appadurai, 2006), to ask critical questions about the systems and practices that shape their lives, and to imagine— through research—how they might be otherwise. Rooted in the activist call "No research on us, without us," CPAR projects reposition those who have traditionally been the objects of study—children, youth, communities under siege, survivors of state or interpersonal violence, immigrants, strug- gling farmers, people in prison, LGBTQIA+ young adults, workers, mothers, educators—as coresearchers, sitting alongside traditionally trained researchers, crafting the questions, methods, analyses, and research products. This commitment to "research with" is an epistemological, ethical, and method- ological critique and transformation of research in which PhD-credentialed

https://doi.org/10.1037/0000241-001
Essentials of Critical Participatory Action Research, by M. Fine and M. E. Torre

researchers (too often well resourced and White) from "outside" gather "data" from communities (too often disinvested in and of color) and then analyze and publish results with little sense of accountability to or response-ability for the people or communities about whom they are writing (Montgomery & bergman, 2017). CPAR is a modest move to democratize and decolonize research as praxis with communities under siege, one dedicated to research that bends toward action (Smith, 1999).

We consider this book a back-pocket guide rather than a "how to." We offer an introduction, an orientation, to the commitments and practices that ground the approach that we hope you will make your own in your specific contexts. We write from our positions at The Public Science Project and Critical Psychology doctoral program at the Graduate Center of the City University of New York where we have participated in a range of CPAR projects for 25 years—in prisons and schools, with high school students, college students, women experiencing domestic violence, asylum-seeking families separated at the border and detained within the United States, and community members in the Bronx and Brooklyn fighting against aggressive policing and gentrification and for urban farming and community control of their culturally responsive schools and local resources (Cammarota & Fine, 2008). With coresearchers, we write to change policy, support organizing, educate the public, re-present communities often misrepresented by scholarship or media, and build theory. In this book, we sketch images of how deeply decentralized and critical research has been undertaken with communities and offer some examples, making visible the questions we have asked ourselves and the communities with whom we collaborate, the decisions and mistakes we have made. If you are looking for a methods book with an atheoretical or ahistoric formula or algorithm, put the book down now—you will be disappointed. If, however, you are willing to think through the deeply contextual and relational critical science questions, commitments, and processes involved in researching with communities on issues of profound, intimate, and urgent concern, drawing on a range of methods, with humility and the skills you likely already have, read on.

We write this volume in the midst of a pandemic and a time of unending state and interpersonal violence against people of color—African Americans and immigrants. At the same time, we witnessed inspiring uprisings, led largely by young people of color and joined by allies from across racial and ethnic groups, ages, genders, and sexualities, informed by evidence gathered bottom up. We all know the names of wealthy White people impacted by COVID-19 who have been reported on in the news, but we will never publicly hear the names of the "essential workers" and their family members who have taken ill, the people in prison who have died of COVID, the children in detention camps and youth or adults in prisons, on the streets, and in public housing who are also impacted—and at staggeringly higher rates—but without tests, without a vaccine, without health care, the hundreds of thousands deemed not newsworthy. The virus has only exacerbated and made hypervisible long-standing inequalities that have built and defined our nation. We all witnessed the state-sanctioned slaughter of George Floyd and learned of the murder of Breonna Taylor and so many other African Americans killed by police. For some of us, this was news; for others, the killings echoed stories our grandmothers warned us about. As we bear witness to state-sanctioned violence against Black, Native, and immigrant communities, we must reckon with the fact of our deeply unequal connections. We must reveal and contend with the policies and structures that intimately link us, that breed and legitimate inequities that create and inflate privileges for some of us, that simultaneously produce brutality for others of us. CPAR is an approach to psychological research in which research collectives intentionally investigate these power differentials and inequities that hide under the banner of "normality" as part of their methodological praxis. Wisdom and care, vulnerabilities and points of view, are exchanged across diverse experiences and standpoints, through participatory inquiry, purposefully guided by those who are most impacted, as a humble gesture toward knowledge justice (de Sousa-Santos, 2014).

Our goal in this volume is to be as clear as possible about our values and decisions in design, analysis, writing, and the actions that grow from our critical inquiry. We are not saying to do it this way or follow the exact steps we have taken. Instead, we offer, throughout the text, moments to pause for CPAR reflections—questions, ethical considerations, epistemological commitments—for research collectives to take up in relation to their particular contexts. While we hope our work speaks to a broad audience, in many ways, we are writing with special attention to those located in universities who yearn to build research collaboratively and respectfully with communities outside the academy. It is to graduate students and faculty that we share these considerations, commitments, and questions as a way to help you deepen inclusion and participation on your research teams and with those who participate in your studies, to encourage you to get beneath the dominant stories and bring to the surface important counter-narratives and knotty contradictions in your work, to provide strategies for developing accessible analyses for widespread dissemination and provocation, and to create pathways for you to move your collaborative research toward action.

CPAR is shaped in conversation and dialogue, across lines of power and difference, and in ways that are deeply contextual and relational. Like any good GPS, we will help you think through where you are beginning and where you want to end and then offer a set of possible routes toward just research.

WHY CPAR? CRITICAL ELEMENTS

CPAR offers a way to think about how, with whom, and for whom we design research, analyze our findings, and disseminate results. The research sits atop a heavy existential, political, and ethical question: To whom are we—as researchers, often but not always based in universities—accountable? This question anchors all CPAR projects, particularly in times of crisis.

The acronym CPAR reflects the critical elements and values that underlie this approach. The *C* stands for critical, which means that our projects are rooted in a range of social theories focused on questions of power, structural and intimate violence, and inequities and that our projects are shaped by a collective anchored by those most impacted by injustice. Criticality materializes in our theoretical perspectives and our research collectives. Theoretically, CPAR projects draw from a range of critical perspectives: critical race, feminist, poststructural, decolonial, disability, Marxist, Indigenous, and/or queer theory. In terms of our research collectives, our designs are developed around questions of power and inequity, in collaboration and dialogue with those most affected by injustice. This line of vision—built from everyday lived experience with the policies and conditions under study—widens our understandings of the shape of the problem, expands the kinds of evidence and methods necessary to document inequities, and influences how and to whom we choose to present our findings in the larger world.

There are many variations of participatory action research (PAR), as elaborated later in this book, in which children, youth, elders, and others engage with academics as coresearchers. An important distinction is that CPAR focuses intentionally on questions of power and injustice, intersectionality and action. We view critical research as one more resource in, by, and for movements for justice.

As in all PAR projects, the *P* in CPAR stands for rich and deep participation by a collective of researchers, including and centered on those most impacted by the issue being studied. Optimally, a diverse research collective is involved throughout: in theorizing, crafting research questions and designs, figuring out methods and samples, conducting analysis, and writing up the findings. As you will see in Chapters 2 and 3, however, it is not enough to "invite" "diverse" people into the research team; processes must be engaged so everyone's gifts and lines of vision are visible and animated, and all forms of privilege (e.g., academic, White, highly educated) are checked.

The *A* signals that CPAR projects link research with action through a range of forms: scholarship, social policy, teaching, legal reform, organizing, and sometimes theatre, spoken word, graphic arts, comics, digital shorts, music, and more. The overall aim of most projects is to build theory from the ground up, advance social change, reeducate the public, and provoke to action both people in our communities and those who bear witness.

The *R* represents a commitment to systematic inquiry—qualitative, quantitative, and/or mixed methods; historical and visual; creative and traditional—undertaken as democratic knowledge production, centered in the perspectives of those most silenced.

In many ways, CPAR is like other approaches to research. As you will see in Chapters 2, 3, and 4, we begin with theoretical frameworks drawn from existing literatures but always in lively conversation and contestation with other social and cultural ways of knowing, as well as the diverse and textured standpoints and experiences of our research team members. Together, we engage in *collective reflexivity* to explore how our biographies and experiences inform how we see the issue at hand, share questions, and develop designs, analyses, and writing. We unpack our individual and collective perspectives and the emotions we carry into the inquiry. We address and try to tease apart our differences, questioning perspectives borne through hegemonic privilege and oppression. We attend closely to the perspectives of those who have most endured unjust conditions. These collective knowledge-building activities allow us to thicken what we know of "the field" and uncover a set of research questions worth asking, questions that prioritize, in the spirit of liberation theologian and social psychologist Ignacio Martín-Baró (1994), justice for the most marginalized.

Once our research questions take shape from our collective deliberations, we craft a design and spend time producing and sharing knowledge within the research group and then beyond. Borrowing from Sandra Harding (1991), we call this *strong objectivity*—the relentless and rigorous bringing together of various points of view, kinds of evidence, and arguments in critical inquiry and dialogue, to ask questions for which we do not yet know the answers. This process itself—as you will see—is humbling, invigorating, at times treacherous, and at others joyful, but it always, we argue, enhances the validity of the research.

As you will read in later chapters, we care about traditional social science commitments, including objectivity, validity, generalizability, reflexivity, and ethics—but with a critical edge. We see these as crucial aspects of the collective project of creating a public science. CPAR research collectives are organized according to the commitment to research as democratic knowledge production. We intentionally expand who is considered an expert and what knowledges hold value. We challenge the presumed exclusive authority of the academically trained researcher and take seriously our response-ability to producing research materials with and for the communities, movements, and/or groups we are working with and alongside.

WHERE COLLECTIVE WISDOM GROWS: PARTICIPATORY CONTACT ZONES

CPAR projects are designed by vibrant and diverse research collectives that include a range of coresearchers. A research collective may include neighborhood residents, activists, lawyers, community leaders, educators, elders, historians, artists, and others who share a passion for the issue of study. We engage these collectives as *participatory contact zones* (Torre, 2009), spaces where differently positioned people come together, with distinct relationships to power and vulnerability, where our differences are cultivated as resources. As you will see in our discussion of CPAR projects throughout the book, within participatory contact zones, dynamics of power and the related inevitable tensions they produce are analyzed and understood as method, as part of (not an interruption of) the research process.

As a research team with different lived experiences, areas of expertise, and comfort with academic skills such as statistics, we read the existing literatures together and contrast the academic literature with what we know from our own biographies, cultures, music, and affects to understand more fully the issue we are studying—whether it be aggressive policing, the overincarceration of people of color, experiences of youth who are pushed out of school, queer youth in schools, young people aging out of foster care while in college, women experiencing domestic violence, families separated at the U.S. border, students of color attending predominantly White universities, or restorative justice. For each project, we host research retreats—or first gatherings—where we collectively paint the landscape of issues we will be researching. We share our distinct standpoints, interview each other about our lives and related experiences, and build on our collective knowledge about our topic, reading and discussing articles, watching short films, watching and/or conducting interviews, searching archives, and reviewing public data. All materials "on topic" that we review together should be accessible to varied literacy levels, languages, and (dis)abilities; in these research retreats, we bring together materials that are academic and popular, historic and contemporary, music and art, written by youth and elders, cultural materials and social media. As we move between our lives and past and contemporary ideas about our topic, we build trust among each other as we encourage dissent and work through our sometimes clashing points of view. We challenge perspectives borne in privilege and seek the buried wisdom that has been silenced in the margins—the knowledge of the "special-ed" rooms, the juvenile justice facilities, the shelters, beneath and inside mental health diagnoses, and detention camps. These conversations are often messy; we bump into each other and sometimes say things that are hurtful. When this happens—and it happens to all of us at one point or another, across all our differences—we apologize, deepen our learning, recommit to each other and our shared goals, and try to keep building valid social inquiry that we move research toward action.

Please note that negotiation of power is part of all research, even in the "lab." The difference is that in conventional research, these conversations are usually unacknowledged. For example, consider graduate students working with faculty who have the final say or are the only ones given credit or large-scale public health research where graduate students conducting research and/or analyses are not recognized. In these cases, rarely are differences respected, aired, or addressed through a lens of power. In CPAR, they are understood as the marrow of CPAR knowledge production.

Our participatory contact zones carve out a "holding environment" (Winnicott, 1973) where we can speak and listen, argue differences and disagreements, develop trust together, stumble, say I am sorry, learn from mistakes, challenge each other, grow new analyses, and build a more critical and imaginative knowledge base—precisely because we dare to inquire together. Members of the collective often establish guiding ethical principles so the contact zone is safe enough: commitments to group practices and research methods and analyses that are antiracist, antisexist, antihomophobic, antixenophobic, anti-Islamophobic, antiableist, and so on, and when someone slips up, we develop processes to acknowledge, question each other, and grow. Engaging power (or Whiteness or elitism, etc.) is not easy. Conflicts do and will surface, even in "participatory" contact zones— see Chapter 3—when traditionally trained researchers engage in critical inquiry with, and not on, individuals and even when research team members "choose" to stand and work together in solidarity. It bears repeating that CPAR is not necessarily a comfortable experience; reflecting on the colonizing history of psychology and research and trying to collaborate across it can be bumpy and challenging, but when tied to the work of creating a different future, it can also be exhilarating.

The commitment to collectivity runs deep, from beginning to end of a CPAR project. On projects with large and small budgets, we are intentional about collective ethics, credit, process, power, money, authorship, child care, transportation, language, food, vulnerabilities to state violence, our purpose, and what actions and audiences we need to address. Coresearchers are compensated for labor and time with combinations of stipends, movie tickets, gift cards, college credits, food, metro cards, child care, translators, and travel funds. In our written work and our videos and online productions, we are all acknowledged as coauthors, and when we present the work, in our various capacities and contexts, everyone gets credit. Our first collective "product" is usually a report, brochure, community event, or policy document designed to give back the evidence or stories and statistics to the community and activists and policymakers or those leading campaigns for change. We also write academic papers together and present at academic and activist conferences. For more detailed images of the work, please visit The Public Science Project (https://www.publicscienceproject.org), where you can look through participatory projects conducted in prisons, schools, and communities; read academic papers; watch youth-created videos; and review legal testimony we have submitted based on our scholarship.

SITUATING CPAR IN THE QUALITATIVE TRADITIONS

CPAR reflects an epistemology, not a methodology. While we are allied with many scholars who work in the qualitative traditions, CPAR signals a distinct way of thinking about who has knowledge, who holds expertise, and how new knowledge can be produced, across differences, when the perspective of those most impacted by injustice are privileged and fueling movements for change are prioritized. CPAR methodologies are often both qualitative and quantitative, visual and creative, and typically closely aligned with a variety of qualitative traditions, including grounded theory (Levitt, 2021), decolonial epistemologies (Smith, 1999), decolonial feminism (Lugones, 2010), intersectionality (Collins, 1991, 2012; Combahee River Collective, 1977; Crenshaw, 2008), and liberation theory (Martín-Baró, 1994). That is, in CPAR, we are interested in how people make sense of the worlds they inhabit and the worlds they make. Participatory researchers collaborate fully and respectfully with communities under siege, rather than gathering top-down narratives.

A basic commitment of CPAR is to create space within the research practice to re-view and challenge the dominant stories being told about the communities, to get underneath the stereotypes and caricatures that populate social science and mainstream media (e.g., about queer youth or women in prison or men who lead a street life or young people arrested by police or school push outs, undocumented college students, teens in foster care). To do that, we create a research community within our team, where we study together—through books, music, memory work, writing—what has been said about (not by) members of these groups. This happens as part of our "literature review" before we finalize our research questions and designs and as part of determining our research purpose.

Within our participatory contact zone, we study together how structural dynamics move under the skin and affect us—all of us (see Fanon, 1952; Lugones, 2010; Quan, 2019; Smith, 1999; Weis & Fine, 2012). Please think about how or when or with whom you enact, embody, are affected by, bear witness to, listen to others in silence, are triggered by, have been wounded by the aggressive entitlements of White privilege, the ways that class formations are racialized, the implicit presumptions of heterosexuality, the widespread evidence of gendered violence, the patronizing of persons with disabilities, or how anti-Muslim or Native or immigrant violence is baked into the rule of law. We say this not to be "politically correct" but for you to understand that none of us is outside these dynamics, and as researchers, we bring these "unthought knowns" into the research if we are not reflexive. Some of us benefit from these dynamics, some are assaulted daily, and some are oblivious. But none of us is outside. Qualitative (and quantitative) inquiry has long been haunted by the unacknowledged privilege of researchers who study "other people" without reflecting on our epistemologies of privilege and ignorance (Mills, 2012). These are dynamics, silences, not-noticings we have grown accustomed to, dynamics CPAR aims to make visible (Lewin, 1951).

CRITICAL EPISTEMOLOGICAL ROOTS: WIDENING OUR UNDERSTANDING OF EXPERTISE

CPAR challenges traditional notions of whose knowledge has value, whose expertise is recognized, whose expertise or ignorance needs to be challenged, and to whom research is accountable. Our work rests on critical scholars, including Anisur Rahman, who, in 1985, argued for participatory research as a form of social liberation:

> Liberation, surely, must be opposed to all forms of domination over the masses. . . . But—and this is the distinctive viewpoint of PAR—domination of masses by elites is rooted not only in the polarization of control over the

means of material production but also over the means of knowledge production including, as in the former case, the social power to determine what is valid or useful knowledge. (p. 119)

At the core of CPAR lies a question: Who is the expert?

In many of our CPAR projects, to open up a conversation about "expertise"— we have asked our coresearchers—youth, people in prison, youth in foster care, communities organized against police violence, LGBTQIA+ young people in schools, immigrant students—to "draw a researcher." And for decades, we have received images that look like Dr. Researchy.

CPAR REFLECTION

Stop reading! Grab a pen and draw a researcher. Just sketch it on that piece of paper beside you. Are they African American? Pregnant? In a wheelchair? From a working-class neighborhood? Or does your researcher look like the one in Figure 1.1?

FIGURE 1.1. Dr. Researchy

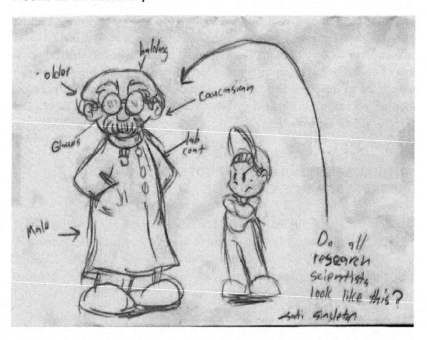

Note. Copyright 2006 by Sati Singleton, Opportunity Gap youth researcher. Reprinted with permission.

The question "Who is the expert?" forces us to think about whose knowledge, language, dialects, forms of speech, intuitions, suspicions, behaviors, clothing, histories, cultural traditions are considered "valid" and whose ways of knowing are considered "biased." CPAR recognizes that all of us possess deep and unique knowledge and understandings of our everyday lives, of the experiences of our families and communities. Because of CPAR's commitment to researching for justice, our research designs bend toward a commitment to prioritizing the knowledge and wisdom of those who live at the radical margins of society; those who have lived the consequences of accumulated dispossession in their schools, from police, at work, from family and kin, or on the streets; and those who have been exiled from the production of social science. CPAR returns those perspectives to their rightful place: to the center of the research.

CPAR REFLECTION

Go to https://www.publicscienceproject.org, search for "Polling for Justice," and watch the video. This video, developed as part of Polling for Justice, a New York City-wide survey of youth by youth, brings Dr. Researchy to life and challenges how we think about who has "expertise" to study "other people's" lives. From the point of view of critical participatory researchers, we all have expertise, and the most valid research brings together diverse perspectives but is rooted in the line of vision narrated by those most vulnerable, who are most impacted by injustice and most attuned to the stings of structural violence.

We realize this stance may destabilize your sense of "Is this science?" This is democratic, public science; inquiry rooted in deep, complex, and bottom-up understandings of significant topics; science created by richly diverse research teams through the systematic gathering of data, numbers and words, statistics and stories, drawn from thoughtfully constructed samples and analyzed in ways both transparent and valid.

DISCIPLINARY ELDERS: HISTORICAL ROOTS IN COMMUNITY-BASED INQUIRY

In this next section of the book, we introduce you to your disciplinary ancestors, those social scientists who long ago worked with and in community, alongside everyday people, documenting the consequences and the origins of social injustice. Many of these scholars and their community-based projects have been whited out of the academy canon. This chapter is a humble attempt to reconstitute some of our academic lineage.

PAR has a long interdisciplinary history—its legacy can be traced to grassroots organizing, popular education, and liberation movements around the globe, in Africa, Asia, and South, Central, and North America (see Cahill et al., 2010; Carolissen et al., 2017; Fals Borda & Rahman, 1991; Hall, 2005; Kapoor & Jordan, 2019; Land, 2015; Maguire, 1987; Zeller-Berkman, 2014, for examples of participatory designs to support local struggles in Canada, Australia, India, Palestine and Israel, New Zealand, the United States, South Africa, Tanzania, and Guatemala, respectively, and linking movements of public science and social justice). In this long tradition, PAR projects excavate subjugated knowledge, challenge stereotypes, reveal structural violence, bear witness to injustice, expose circuits of dispossession and privilege, and provoke an imagination for what else is possible (Fine & Ruglis, 2009). With this in mind, we offer a set of grounding commitments of critical PAR, key features worth preserving.

Democratic Knowledge Production and the Right to Research

Anthropologist Arjun Appadurai (2006) wrote that all people should have the "right to research"—especially those who have been most denied equity and dignity. In CPAR projects, youth and adults marginalized by oppressive systems exercise the right to research and engage in democratic knowledge production even as much of their experience with schools, police, social workers, and public policy has been denied, obscured, or pathologized by social science. Consider the history of the Highlander Folk School, now the Highlander Research and Education Center (https://www.highlandercenter. org), where community research, popular education, literacy campaigns, and music and folklore flourished to document and transform the injustices and build solidarities across the mining communities of the Appalachian Mountains of Tennessee. For instance, at the initiative of coal-mining White housewives who were already collecting incidence records of fathers, husbands, and sons with black lung disease, Highlander brought citizen science together with disabled miners, black-lung physicians, leaders of the United Mine Workers, and musicians to document, in epidemiology and song, the embodied consequences of the coal mining industry. With a blend of science, lived experience, music, and political courage, Highlander has been a mainstay of CPAR and popular education, organizing for justice and gathering for music, joy, community science, and resistance.

CPAR REFLECTION

As we build our research collectives, we must ask, Whose perspectives are missing?

Researchers' Obligation to Document the Consequences of Structural Dispossession

CPAR projects understand that our lives and the conditions within which we live are linked. Rejecting the naive individualism that dominates in psychology, this insight is crucial to participatory research, in what we study, how we study, and the materials we create out of CPAR evidence. In the early 1900s, progressive era sociologist Jane Addams built the Hull House (https://www.hullhousemuseum.org) in Chicago, where poor immigrant and wealthy elite women and men lived together, building lives cooperatively and conducting research on the inequitable health consequences endured by immigrants living in poverty. Addams understood, as a privileged White woman, that elites have an obligation to conduct research with, share shelter with, and struggle for justice with those who have been marginalized. From their living room in Hull House, men and women across social classes collaborated on maps documenting flows of garbage and sanitation in Chicago, tracking employment opportunities available to and withheld from immigrant women, and measuring health care disparities by class and immigrant status. These studies were submitted to the local government and fed to radical organizing groups, rooted in the insight that our collective well-being is threatened if one group suffers.

With similar commitments to solidarity, social psychologist Marie Jahoda, a White North American professor at Columbia University, undertook an ethnographic study of men and women in Marienthal, Austria, in the early 1930s, enduring the devastating consequences of the worldwide economic depression. Jahoda and colleagues from the Institute of Psychology at the University of Vienna joined with community members to document—that is, expose—the material and embodied consequences of massive unemployment on community life, even as they represented community members with dignity and desires for meaningful engagements. They studied health, social relationships, and even the pace at which people walked across the streets. They studied how despair swelled and a sense of hopelessness set into community life. With local activists and residents, Jahoda and colleagues published popular and academic texts, including the text *Marienthal*; translated the research into materials for political organizers; and circulated the materials on a socialist radio program, after which Jahoda was briefly imprisoned (Jahoda et al., 2001).

It should be noted that *Marienthal* is rarely taught in psychology classes, and yet it is such a daring project in which a social scientist lived with, valued, and documented the everyday, embodied, and social consequences of the great depression in a community in Austria that was fully unemployed. Jahoda dedicated her skills as an ethnographer to make visible the dehumanizing consequences of mass economic devastation.

CPAR REFLECTION

How will our research document the contours of power and oppression—the systems and structures, the lived experience, the interconnections between those who benefit and those who suffer?

Researchers' Responsibility to Document the Roots of Injustice

Critical PAR collectives study together the history, policies, and context of the issue being researched, tracing the structural roots of injustice and social and psychological aftermath. CPAR projects study the history and the present and the downstream effects of inequity but also the cumulative privileges that accrue upstream. Perhaps the oldest example of research designed to challenge a downstream gaze comes from the writings of W. E. B. Du Bois.

In the late 1890s, the scholar W. E. B. Du Bois was hired to investigate "the Negro problem" in Philadelphia. He knew the invitation was framed in ways both racist and victim blaming but proceeded, with community members, to systematically map the housing, health, education, and financial conditions in which poor Blacks were managing difficult lives. He meticulously documented how problems in the Black community could be traced back to history, structures, and policies of White supremacy, exclusion, and discrimination. He produced scholarly documents, including *The Philadelphia Negro* (Du Bois, 1899, 1911/2008; Morris, 2018), wrote policy documents and newspaper articles, published a novel, and produced *The Star of Ethiopia*, a pageant to educate the African American public about their history and sociology.

CPAR REFLECTION

From whose perspective is the research framed? How else might this story be told? Whose points of view are being excluded?

Centering the Experience and Standpoints of Those Most Impacted

We are all impacted by systems of injustice, though unevenly. Those living in particularly unjust conditions understand nuances of the injustice that those with more privileged lives do not. As CPAR projects highlight the knowledge and participation of those living in and/or most impacted by the conditions being studied in all aspects of the research, research collectives take seriously the language and framing used by those most familiar with the conditions. In the late 1980s, what became known as the Green Haven Think Tank emerged at Green Haven Prison in New York State. A research team of men in the prison, led by former Black Panther Eddie Ellis, dedicated themselves to investigating and preventing the rising numbers of Black and Latino men consigned to the New York State prison system. Under the direction of Ellis, who was imprisoned for 23 years, and with the quiet help of psychologist Kenneth Clark, the research team—all incarcerated street penologists and members of the (Black) Resurrection and (Latino) Conciencia study groups—designed a study that determined the overwhelming majority of the prison population of New York State came from a small geographic location. Foreshadowing the "superblock" studies, Ellis and colleagues' systematic analysis demonstrated that 85% of the New York State prisoners were Black and Latino, and 75% of them originated in seven neighborhoods in New York City. The Green Haven Think Tank (1997) policy document urged a nontraditional policy analysis of the seven "symbiotic neighborhoods"— Lower East Side, South Bronx, Harlem, Brownsville, Bedford-Stuyvesant, East New York, and South Jamaica—and recommended that the men from these neighborhoods be trained in community development while in prison, and once released, funded to help rebuild the communities they came from through internships, mentoring, and community programs.

Ellis was careful and clever about language—insisting on "person-first" language (i.e., "men who are incarcerated," not "incarcerated men"; "people with disabilities," not "disabled people"). He refused to call prisons part of a "criminal justice system," but instead a "criminal punishment system." The Center for NuLeadership that Ellis formed after his release is a gorgeous example of ongoing collaboration across bars, initiated by men most impacted by the criminal punishment system, recruiting the help of outside researchers but centering the views of those on the inside.

CRAFTING AND PERFORMING PUBLIC-FACING SCHOLARSHIP FOR ACTION, TRANSFORMATION, AND PROVOCATION

CPAR projects are designed to provoke change—whether in policy, attitudes, law, performance, or consciousness. They are designed to spark what existential philosopher Maxine Greene (1977) called "aesthetic openings," not "anesthetic numbing," a "wide awakeness" of how things might be otherwise. CPAR research collectives seek to complicate single stories, widen social consciousness, and be "of use" for policy change. As you will read throughout this volume, some projects produce statistical and narrative evidence for litigation, as in the case of the Morris Justice Project's commitment to gathering community-generated statistical evidence of the cumulative consequences of racialized police violence, specifically of the use of "stop and frisk" under "broken windows" policing in New York City (Stoudt et al., 2016). Other projects gather narratives from women in prison, their children, and their correction officers to convince legislators to fund college in prison. You will read about projects designed to celebrate "out" queer educators and demand protection for their full selves in the classrooms or to convince universities to provide housing for foster students in college or for higher education admissions officers to remove the "box" that formerly incarcerated people are asked to check when applying to college or for jobs. Each project generates distinct materials to "be of use" to community.

Perhaps the most powerful historical reference for why and how psychological research should be dedicated to action, transformation, and provocation comes from El Salvador, where social psychologist Ignacio Martín-Baró labored with colleagues, farmers, miners, workers, religious leaders, activists, and community members to create science by and for the people (Martín-Baró, 1994). In 1982, Martín-Baró returned from graduate school at the University of Chicago to El Salvador to initiate a series of "people's" research projects at Universidad Centroamericana, where he was the director of the University Institute for Public Opinion. Building a series of public surveys whose results served as a "social mirror" reflecting the collective lived reality of the poor, Martín-Baró argued that praxis of research of and by "the people" could create a powerful tool to "challenge the official lies" of the authoritarian government. He and five colleagues were murdered by a counterinsurgency unit of the Salvadoran government elite, backed by the United States in November of 1989.

CPAR REFLECTION

To whom is our research accountable? How might the research challenge the "official lies" and help to provoke an imagination for what else is possible? What kinds of evidence are needed to provoke wide-awakenings?

With the epistemological foundations of CPAR and a grounding study in your mind, we turn now to the questions of how: How to build research teams with meaningful diversity, how to design knowledge sharing and systematic inquiry to lift up a range of perspectives, how to cultivate an ethical framework for collaboration, how to analyze in ways both participatory and valid, how to write together, and how to create public-facing scholarship of meaning and provocation.

2 PARTICIPATORY DESIGN

Critical participatory action research (CPAR) enacts an ethical, relational, and complicated commitment to research with people, communities, and movements. At root, CPAR requires processes that are integral to qualitative inquiry: careful and active listening; critical self-reflexivity; theoretical frameworks porous enough that narratives can be coconstructed in dialogue; ongoing analyses and negotiations of power, privilege, and vulnerabilities; and courage to offer interpretations of expansive material about living in the world. As we note throughout the book, the research collaboratives that drive CPAR projects generally and intentionally bring together people who are quite differently positioned in relation to the issue or dynamic they are studying. Building on the work of Mary Louise Pratt (1991) and Gloria Anzaldúa (1987, 2002), with a desire to engage power and solidarity, we have found it useful to think about these collectives as participatory contact zones (Torre, 2009), sites for building research from a "collective we"—what Anzaldúa calls *"nos-otras,"* holding the tensions of entangled "us" and "others." Here, we present one study—What's Your Issue?—to anchor our discussion of research design.

https://doi.org/10.1037/0000241-002
Essentials of Critical Participatory Action Research, by M. Fine and M. E. Torre

ASSEMBLING A DIVERSE COMMUNITY OF CORESEARCHERS

What's Your Issue? (WYI) was a national participatory study, part interview project, part ethnography, part online survey completed by more than 6,000 LGBTQIA+ young people around the United States, deliberately oversampling youth of color and those considered "hard to reach." We documented the experiences, dreams, and desires of LGBTQIA+ young people from every state in the country, Puerto Rico, and Guam. Our research collective originally included four academically trained adult researchers (with a range of racial and ethnic identities, genders, and sexualities) and soon thereafter expanded to include a dedicated, paid research team of 40 LGBTQIA+ young people—activists, organizers, students, and artists—drawn from across the United States.

Our first research collective retreat was held for 3 days on Fifth Avenue and 34th Street in New York City at The Public Science Project in the City University of New York (CUNY) Graduate Center. Participants were 40 young people, aged 15 to 22, from regional teams in 10 communities who identified as queer, lesbian, gay, trans, undocumented, "refusing these categories," Chicana, White, African American, Creole, Korean American, Jewish, "a mutt," Black-Japanese, and "changing all the time" from Seattle, Detroit, Boston, St. Louis, Jackson (MS), Jersey City (NJ), New York City, Los Angeles, New Orleans, and Tucson (AZ). Most identified as "of color," lesbian, gay, bisexual, transgender, inquiring, asexual, and/or gender fluid or gender expansive. From their distinct communities and biographies, they brought essential—and vastly distinct—buckets of wisdom to our inquiry.

Our task was to build an intergenerational research team, engage in dialogues about the joyful and difficult aspects of growing up LGBTQIA+ and gender expansive in different parts of the country, generate research questions, review "traditional survey items," generate original survey items, conduct local ethnographies in our home communities, and create an online survey that would reach young people across the country, aged 14 to 24, who identify as LGBTQIA+. For the survey, we wanted to attract a sample that would be racially and ethnically diverse and geographically dispersed and that identified with a wide range of experiences of gender, inclusive of young people who were too often left out of typically school-based, national "samples"—precariously housed, involved with juvenile justice, in school and out, with and without disabilities, wealthy and not. We decided that the survey itself would be mixed methods, comprising closed-ended quantitative items to understand the scale and distribution of social inequities confronting LGBTQIA+ young people (e.g., health, family relations, interactions with police, and schooling), short open-ended prompts (e.g., Describe yourself in five words or How would you describe your gender? Sexuality? Race and ethnicity?), and a range of longer open-ended questions (e.g., Tell us about your proudest moment, Where do you find community? Where do you hope to be in 5 years?) to open a narrative window into the depth and heterogeneity of experiences and dreams within this community. Our task was to document the landscape of LGBTQIA+ experiences through the intersectional lens of race and ethnicity, gender, sexuality, (dis)ability, immigration status, and geography, with attention to struggles, relationships, institutional encounters, dreams, activisms, and solidarities.

In WYI, members of the research collective were recruited from a national network of LGBTQIA+ youth organizations. To build our "we" (our participatory contact zone), we invited the 10 regional teams to New York City. In our first hours together, we interviewed each other, drew identity maps (described more thoroughly at the end of this chapter), and described and shared meaningful artifacts and photos we brought from home. We created a living and growing list of ethical commitments we would hold with each other and within our research. We reviewed standardized instruments and interview protocols that had been used to study LGBTQIA+ youth and then asked, "What might we want to adapt?" "What kinds of questions do we want to be sure ask LGBTQIA+ young people?" and "What kinds of questions do we wish had been asked in previous studies?"

With a commitment to ground our research in the wide-ranging experiences and cumulative wisdom of our coresearchers, we talked through the lived intersections of everyday life and our different racialized and regionalized experiences with police, schools, health care centers, housing, mental illness, activism, our families, books, films, and music. Over time, as we grew more comfortable sharing, our collective sense of purpose also grew. The research collective felt an accountability to produce works of meaning to support the next generation of young people just beginning to ask questions about gender, sexuality, race and ethnicity, and being Mormon or intersex, living on a farm, being Latinx or the child of evangelicals, and so on.

We decided to interview each other again in more detail and create short, accessible videos of our biographies of relationships, desires, racism and homophobia, activism, and wounds. In their interview, Shéár Avory, one of the coresearchers and a national social justice youth activist who identifies as a trans Black Indigenous femme from Los Angeles, narrated the devastating consequences of the "cradle-to-prison" pipeline encountered by queer young people of color:

> From age 5 to 10, my father had me in conversion therapy. When that didn't work, I was placed in foster care at 10. I never finished high school because I was traumatically bullied in elementary, middle, and high school. At 17, I left

LA for NYC. I wasn't able to find stable housing and was finally thrown out of a youth shelter because they wouldn't let me stay with my partner. We were on the streets; went to a small home in rural Pennsylvania to stay with relatives, and then there was family violence—it's Trump country. We ended up in jail— I was assigned to the men's facility and experienced relentless transphobia— me at 18, being lectured by a [police] captain about chromosomes X and Y.

This is, of course, one story, but the connections to and experiences of family, school, family violence, and jail resonated with many. As part of our research gatherings, we shared our dreams and desires, disagreements, and painful moments. We exchanged stories about what we do when we need help, how we support ourselves, and how we can support each other. We delicately entered a conversation about mental health, depression, and suicide. Kat, a coresearcher who identifies as Black and a survivor from Detroit REPRESENT! told the story of her experiences with foster care, homelessness, and activism:

My experiences "in the system" encouraged me to become the change I needed when I was younger. I was in the system since I was 13; ran away, lived on the streets, in shelters, juvenile facilities, back into sleeping in an abandoned building. Then I met [an organizer] who offered me a place to stay, and I learned the importance of activism and giving back. So now, as an activist and an organizer, I work on campaigns for housing, against domestic violence, and for the human rights of young people living on the streets of Detroit.

Each young person reflected on the winding path to late adolescence and their relentless attempts to be recognized and whole. Together we read articles and poetry about and by young people who identify as "queer"—the language our coresearchers prefer. As we swapped stories, we started to notice a sad and beautiful pattern: Incidents of intimate betrayal were followed by a generous and collective response of care. Queer youth in Detroit who were thrown out of their homes by families or had fled mobilized a fierce and loving response: They created a housing co-op in an abandoned building to give themselves and each other shelter. Korean American Christian lesbians and trans youth in Seattle were being evicted from the homes of their families of origin because of gender and sexuality issues. They established a hotline to support gender-expansive gay and lesbian youth, some seeking immigration assistance, some desperate to exit from evangelical communities, and others worried about the well-being of little brothers and sisters left behind. This pattern, faintly legible in our early sessions, grew more pronounced throughout the study. The day after we discussed structural violence and intimate betrayals, other stories of care, resistance, tears, and activism would be introduced.

We educated each other about local conditions: the criminalization of LGBTQIA+ young people in New Orleans, housing instability in Detroit, struggles with immigration and U.S. Immigration and Customs Enforcement in Tucson. Stories traveled across sites: Stories of betrayal and surprising solidarities, bold activism, intimate generosities, wounds, dreams, and desires encouraged sections, categories, and individual questions for the survey. Our dialogues forced us to create a survey that was wide open, inviting, accepting, and affirming.

CPAR REFLECTION

Before you design your research project (whether the methods are interviews, surveys, focus groups, and/or visual materials), hold collective space and take time for the research collective to explore the full range of experiences, expertise, and gifts in the room, tracking encounters with injustice, fierce and quiet strategies of coping and resistance, wounds and pleasures, nightmares and dreams.

In our experiences, across regions of the country, we could hear how queer lives—maybe all lives—entangle with policies, structures, and relationships. Young people are both assigned identities and forge their own. Stories of growth and pain are often laced with resistance and relationship. Experiences of discrimination are often launchpads for activism.

Steeped in our own complexity and now tasked with creating a design for a national sample, we understood we needed an instrument that would honor and recognize, invite and appreciate respondents' experiences, an instrument that could capture wounds and dreams, points of oppression, and activism. We wanted to invite a wide range of narratives from young people across regions, race and ethnicity, experiences, biographies, living situations, socioeconomic status, gender, sexualities, immigrant status, and (dis)abilities.

CPAR REFLECTION

When, in interviews, you hear stories of oppression, listen to the words shared, and imagine beyond and remember the person as a whole creative being. Ask how people cope and resist. Ask how they support each other. In big ways and small, it is crucial to capture the creativity and desires for freedom, dignity, and recognition, especially in conditions of severe injustice.

DESIGNING MIRRORS AND WINDOWS

Early in our first 3-day retreat, we read aloud an interview with the writer Junot Díaz in which he spoke about vampires and mirrors:

> You know how vampires have no reflections in the mirror? . . . If you want to make a human being a monster, deny them, at the cultural level, any reflection of themselves. And growing up, I felt like a monster in some ways. I didn't see myself reflected at all. I was like, "Yo, is something wrong with me?" That the whole society seems to think that people like me don't exist? And part of what inspired me was this deep desire, that before I died, I would make a couple of mirrors. That I would make some mirrors, so that kids like me might see themselves reflected back and might not feel so monstrous for it. (Stetler, 2009, para. 2)

And then we wrote. We wrote letters to our younger selves about a time when we felt like vampires and a time when we felt recognized. We talked together, in small groups and large, about what it would mean to create a national survey—of quantitative items, as well as open-ended qualitative questions—that might feel like a mirror to 14- to 24-year-old LGBTQIA+ and gender expansive young people and a window into their struggles, vibrant subjectivities, and the rich complexity of their lives all over the country.

CPAR REFLECTION

It is not enough to recruit a diverse research team; we must build in activities and research practices that keep us all complex, vulnerable, knowing, and open to new perspectives.

Generating rich and valid knowledge that resonates beyond dominant communities and experiences takes more than creating "diverse" research collectives. Collectives must intentionally engage intersectional dialogues about the colonial extractive history of research in marginalized communities, purposefully exposing the ways Whiteness and privilege has undermined democratic knowledge production, from the structural discrimination and privileging within the academy to the interpersonal affirmations and dismissals that told us that some of us were "smart" and others of us were "weird," "not normal," and "not very smart." CPAR research collective spaces should be ones where members can show and learn who is funny, who is an artist, who has great mathematical talents, who has "style," who has a sharp racial critique, who aches, who holds too many in their heart, and how our mosaic can build research.

To cultivate a diverse, respectful, and critical community of scholars from the mosaic, CPAR projects have developed a series of critical practices designed to animate the gifts we each bring, make visible the experiential knowledge of each coresearcher, and build a provisional sense of trust among the research team, recognizing that our coresearchers contribute different levels of academic comfort and alienation.

IMAGES OF OPENING SESSIONS

Next, we try to capture some of our "first meetings" on varied CPAR projects to stimulate your imagination for how you might design research spaces to explore the gifts, challenge the hierarchies, find sweet commonalities, build ethics, and only then generate research designs and questions. These first meetings are foundational for unleashing wisdom, concerns, and desires from a range of people, including children, youth, adults, and seniors, in a range of places, including prisons, schools, community centers, detention centers, libraries, and parks. When we begin a research project, we usually engage what McClelland and Fine (2008) called *methodological release points*—that is, methodologies that invite, release, and enable the expression of bold and quiet thoughts, experiences, and affects from a broad range of individuals about the topic of common concern, with the assurance that we are all learning and there are no right answers. Consider two projects and their opening research gatherings.

FOSTERing Growth: Young People in the Foster-Care-to-College Pipeline

After CUNY committed to support and house foster youth interested in pursuing college, the W. T. Grant Foundation funded a small PAR project with foster youth at CUNY. The project started with a simple question: "What are the experiences, opportunities, and obstacles confronted by foster youth in college?" I (MF), along with Professor Katie Cumiskey and Katie's College of Staten Island students, flooded various CUNY campuses with flyers that were created by a team of college students who were formerly in foster care:

ARE YOU A STUDENT OF CUNY WHO HAS BEEN IN THE FOSTER CARE SYS-TEM? IF SO, YOU MUST HAVE SUPER POWERS! JOIN US AS A RESEARCHER TO GATHER STORIES OF STRENGTH and STRUGGLE! Be a Paid Researcher on FOSTER-ing Growth in College!

Katie and I held a dinner, and close to 30 undergraduates showed up, largely community college and 4-year college undergraduates who were in or formerly in the foster care system. Everyone was paid and received a metro card with round trip subway fare. This first meeting was called to explore the range of issues foster youth confront, carry, and cope with and resolve in college; animate the wisdom that youth "in the system" develop; and see who might want to join as a youth researcher.

After a warm-up activity, I tried to explain participatory research—that everyone around the table would be coresearchers, not study "subjects," if they decided to join us. My notes from the evening reflect some of the skepticism in the room:

> Not clear they believed me. Jackets stayed on, some heads on table. "We still get paid, right, for tonight, either way?" I continued, "Yes, yes, you get paid even if you don't hang out for all the research. If you were in foster care, and then you came to CUNY, we are very interested in your wisdom. You know things that we obviously don't. We are hopefully doing this research with you to help the next generation of foster youth coming into CUNY. We need this project to be rooted in your wisdom, so we can create programs, or maybe we'll design an app for new foster youth trying to navigate CUNY."

After pizza and drinks were consumed, names and preferred pronouns traded, I continued,

> I have friends—and a son—who grew up in foster care. They think it's amazing that you're in college. So, we want to be able to understand how you got here and what CUNY needs to do to keep you in school. I know it hasn't been a straight line. I know it's been bumpy, but somehow you were determined. And I know we aren't a group of artists! But can you each make a map of your journey to college? Use red for what got in the way, green for people or opportunities that helped you, and purple to represent your wonderful personal spirit and drive. And then we'll share.

Within 20 minutes, jackets were coming off, and our community room was abuzz with life. "When you're done, just hang your map on the wall. You don't need to put your name—but you can if you want." Thirty maps were posted around the room, like a museum. We invited them to do a "gallery walk" and then asked young people to speak at their tables about what they noticed—connections, surprises, variations, tears, laughter, and struggles.

We asked whether anyone would talk through their map. A young person who introduced themselves as Branch, "Black, queer, and fabulous," explained,

> So, foster care is my red, my green, and my purple! Red because foster care sucks, right? How many of you had food locked in the refrigerator? [15 hands] How many of you were beaten 'cause you didn't want to go to the foster

parents' church? [Eight hands] How many of you had to run away because you were queer? [Five hands] But foster care is also my green because I met the coolest people and purple because, well, frankly, I AM FOSTER CARE!

Branch took a twirl and a bow and received a roomful of applause. After Branch opened the emotional and complicated floodgates, hands were raised, and drawings were layered with laughter and extra slices of pizza. People were sharing their tattoos, embodied archives of their surviving too many systems to put on a map. In the second half of the session, they started to develop the app for incoming foster youth at CUNY. It is always thrilling and predictable that young researchers come alive when they are asked to produce resources for younger people in similar circumstances coming up behind them.

The room broke into three subgroups created on the spot analytic categories spontaneously conceived: How to find free things in New York City—shelter, books, clothes, food, online textbooks, health care; how to report unethical behavior and actions by foster families; and a 24/7 free therapy hotline run by former foster youth. The evening birthed our collective project, FOSTERing Growth: Studying the Needs and Desires of Young People in the Foster-Care-to-College Pipeline (https://www.publicscienceproject.org), which included a participatory design, lasting over 2 years, of longitudinal interviews with a small set of students who were formerly in foster care and focus groups with larger samples. The findings were delivered to the university; some of the foster youth have become coresearchers on other projects, and some dropped out, given life and the pressures of managing college when precariously housed. A beta model of the app was developed.

Changing Minds: The Impact of College in Prison

In the early 1990s, we were working with a few women who were pursuing PhDs while incarcerated at Bedford Hills Correctional Facility. Then, in 1994, President Bill Clinton signed legislation that barred people attending college while in prison access to the noncompetitive Pell grants that supported college-in-prison programs. Within 6 months, nearly all of the 350 college-in-prison programs in the nation shuttered. The eight that survived had to create whole new designs to be sustained without federal support. Women at Bedford Hills Correctional Facility asked us to work with them to resurrect college (with a new college-consortium volunteer model). Soon after it was up and running, the women who helped build it recognized a need to empirically document the impact of college on the women, their children, the prison environment, and their postrelease outcomes. They asked us to evaluate it, and we suggested a CPAR design—a research collective, half of which were women in prison and half from the Graduate Center.

The women on the college committee were excited about a participatory design because it reflected their collaborative organizing efforts, and the Superintendent signed off on it. Our first task was to build a research team that included women who were imprisoned and those who were not (see Fine et al., 2021). We had no funding but much motivation to capture and build collective knowledge about why college matters, grounded in the wisdom of the women about the wretched dehumanization of prison and the transformative possibilities enabled by college behind bars.

To build a research team that would bring together the wide range of perspectives within and outside prison, about college in prison, we offered a course on qualitative research methods in the new college program where, again, we were able to build trust and develop a common language and a set of skills and relationships and also discern key questions—from those who knew best—to shape the final research design. In a class of 15, taught by two then doctoral students, Rosemarie Roberts and Melissa Rivera, each student pursued a qualitative interview with five other women about a question of her own creation. The questions themselves were a beautiful montage, grounded in the women's heterogeneous experiences: What is the impact of college on your children? How does college change how you feel about religion? How do women who have experienced violence all their lives now see their own intellectual signatures? What kinds of poetry do you write in your cell? What is rehabilitation? Why are women sent to solitary? You will notice that the women pursued questions that invited wide open responses. We talked about "good" and "bad" questions, and they were determined to avoid yes/no questions or questions that might suggest judgment or stigma or questions that might elicit a sense of guilt or shame. They were not searching for "right answers" but coconstructing an archive of previously silenced stories. By the end of the course, we had 75 interviews, and seven of the students signed up to join the research team.

The research collective met every other week for 4 years in the College Bound office located in the basement of the prison, and together we shaped the research questions, methods, samples, analysis, and later, the range of scholarly, policy, and public-facing products that resulted from our findings. Our collective knowledge shaped what would ultimately become the study Changing Minds: The Impact of College in Prison (https://www.prisonpolicy. org/scans/changing_minds.pdf). We were clear from the beginning that we wanted to honor the experiences of women inside who were pursuing education, encourage legislators to support federal and state funding for college in prison, and restore Pell grants. After much collaborative deliberation, our final design was organized around questions, methods, samples, and outcomes (see Table 2.1).

TABLE 2.1. Research Design for Changing Minds Study: Questions, Methods, Samples, and Outcomes

Research questions	Method	Sample	Outcomes
1. What are the costs of providing or withholding college in prison?	1. Reincarceration analysis 2. Cost-benefit analysis	$n = 274$ women in college $n = 2,031$ women not in college	Costs of imprisonment Costs of college education Costs of reincarceration
2. What is the impact of college in prison on the safety and management of the prison environment?	3. Surveys of faculty 4. Interviews with corrections officers and administrators	$n = 33$ $n = 6$	Changes in prison disciplinary environment Prison climate Corrections officers' views of and experiences with college in prison Attitudes of women not in the college program about college Faculty views of the college program
3. What are the personal and social effects of college in prison on students and their children?	5. One-on-one interviews conducted by inmate-researchers 6. Focus groups with inmates, children, university presidents, and faculty	$n = 65$ Focus groups: $n = 43$ (inmates) $n = 20$ (faculty) $n = 9$ (children) $n = 7$ (presidents)	Academic persistence and achievement Personal transformation Expression of responsibility for crime and for future decision Reflection on choices made in the past and decisions to be made in the future Civic engagement and participation in prison and outside
4. What is the impact of the college experience on the transition home from prison?	7. In-depth interviews with former inmates 8. Student narratives 9. Reincarceration analysis of former inmates who attended college while in prison	$n = 20$ $n = 18$ $n = 274$ (college students) $n = 2,031$ (women not in college)	Reincarceration rates Economic well-being Health Civic participation Persistence in pursuing higher education postrelease Relations with family and friends

All our methods were cofacilitated by a woman inside and a woman outside, except for interviews with officers and women who had been released. Seeking a full understanding of the impact of college in the prison, we purposefully sought a range of experiences and (counter)stories, gathering narratives from college students, program leaders, those who dropped out, women in the English as a Second Language program, college faculty and presidents, children with mothers in college, corrections officers, and those who were skeptical about the program. As you will see in Chapter 5, all the interview and focus group transcripts were analyzed and interpreted collaboratively.

Across these projects, whether we were studying with foster youth at CUNY or with women in college in prison, our designs were formed in intentional spaces where we explored each others' gifts, experiences, wisdom, wounds, worries, and questions. As coresearchers draw wisdom from experience, place this knowledge in the middle of the room, wrestle with the academic and popular literature and other standpoints in the room, and engage creatively, a series of research questions rise to the surface.

METHODOLOGICAL RELEASE POINTS: STRATEGIES FOR UNLEASHING COLLECTIVE WISDOM

As noted earlier in this chapter, when building a research collective, it is essential to design activities—*methodological release points*—that surface the wisdom that each person carries: the stories, skills, dreams, networks, and gifts, especially for those who assume "I don't have much to offer." There are many wonderful places to look for strategies, from popular education to participatory design practices. The following is a sample of some strategies we have used:

- Draw a researcher. This strategy opens a discussion about the history and politics of research—who gets to be an expert, how communities have been treated, whose knowledge is valued.

- Collective film critics. Watch a film, a documentary, or media clips connected to the issues being studied. Stop periodically and ask everyone to write down critical questions. Use the questions to discuss and build theory from the collective.

- Problem trees. Commonly used in popular education, problem trees allow groups to make connections between everyday experiences and the social or political structures that produce and support them (see Torre & Fox, 2020). Using the metaphor of a tree, the group discusses the following questions: What are the root causes? What holds the trunk that makes the problem so sturdy? Who is dangling from the branches, and what is on the leaves (the symptoms and the resistance)?

- Scavenger hunts. Create a literal scavenger hunt, whereby people can use their specific knowledge and experiences to reframe their transnational wisdoms, experiences with "systems," and their pain, wounds, and betrayals as sources of knowledge rather than scars to be hidden. For instance, in a university, find six books by Latinx queer poets; look at hallway bulletin boards and write down who feels central to this campus and who feels marginal; how do people with physical disabilities navigate the campus; what topics would feel unsafe to discuss here?

- Walking tours. Have members of the group take others on walking tours to expand their understandings and share in the experience of the area, issue, or context.

- Letters to a younger self. It is often useful and beautiful to have young people write letters to themselves as a younger self during a time of struggle, inviting them to articulate how they coped and notice how much strength they mustered to get by. Ask volunteers to read the letters aloud. These letters often elicit new questions.

- Identity mapping. Identity mapping (Futch & Fine, 2014) is a useful method for coresearchers to introduce and re-present their many selves, their wisdom, knowledge, burdens, and imagination. Just after 9/11, in a small critical participatory study with Muslim American youth (Sirin & Fine, 2008), we gave Muslim American teens in the New Jersey and New York areas a simple prompt: "Draw your many selves. Your daughter or son self, religious, school, secret, athletic, musical, religious, friend— all the parts of you." We got rich—but strikingly distinct—portraits of Muslim American adolescents' social and psychological responses to the War on Terror at home. See Figure 2.1 for examples.

- Remixing popular culture. We sometimes bring in cartoons, memes, poetry, or graphs and ask differently positioned youth to interpret what these are trying to say or create a spoken word response to reveal the range of perspectives in the room.

To close out this section, we remind you that these strategies should not be dismissed as icebreakers or gimmicks; they are not "cute" or preliminary

FIGURE 2.1. "Identity Maps" Produced by Muslim American Youth, Circa 2006, in Response to the Question "Draw Your Many Selves"

Note. From *Muslim American Youth: Understanding Hyphenated Identities Through Multiple Methods* (p. 12), by S. R. Sirin and M. Fine, 2008, New York University Press. Copyright 2008 by New York University. Reprinted with permission.

to the "real" research. As methodological release points, they are qualitative research methods that open opportunities to hear and see, from and with, people who experience the issues under study. They create accessible entry points for diverse groups of people to share, build, and deepen their collective knowledge as researchers about the landscape of struggle, opportunity, pain, and desire they are investigating (see Luttrell, 2020). This process is essential before developing research questions or full designs. The insights that surface with these strategies help to build new lenses of analysis and reveal how much our psychological canon has missed, both in terms of how structures, history, institutions, and relationships impinge on individuals and how much people resist, organize, build care worlds, and create new ones—even, or especially, in impossible situations.

A CAUTIONARY NOTE ON PRIVILEGE IN THE CONTACT ZONE

The last point is on building a "we" across power lines, and here we address privilege; Whiteness; and those of us who come from wealth, are well educated, or have enjoyed lives relatively free of economic, racial, and social stressors. That may be most of our readers or some or just a few. Many of us have a strand of privilege in our intersectional bodies that is woven alongside marginalized identities. We are speaking to that line of privilege. In CPAR, privilege is not something to be ashamed of, but it is an opportunity for humility, to learn, and to be response-able. Let us explain.

Each of you reading this book has a distinct way of seeing and making sense of the world—that is, you are and we are "positioned," as feminist philosopher of science Sandra Harding (1991) would say, in a standpoint that emerges at the intersection of our multiple selves. It seems obvious to say that you probably have a standpoint that differs from the person who served you lunch or cleans the bathrooms in your building or sits on the board of trustees. In the wisdom of Audre Lorde (1984), Kimberle Crenshaw (1989), and Patricia Hill Collins (1991, 2012), we know that all of us, and each of you, is positioned somewhere and is also richly intersectional. In fact, you are complex, a person with multiple intersecting identities, some shifting over time, some that come alive, and some that hang back in differing contexts, relationships, and spaces. You bring all of this—the gorgeous and the troubling—into the participatory contact zone. You have an obligation to check the insidious influence of privilege, domination, and silencing within the research collective.

We offer next a few strategies that are useful for interrogating power dynamics in our research collectives, for lifting up counterstories, and for creating democratic processes for collective knowledge building:

- Build processes to check power dynamics. Make sure that those with relative privilege (educational, wealth, Whiteness, able-bodiedness, gender, or just acting entitled) do not talk too much, take over the discussion, or overly influence the questions, frameworks, and instruments. Do not interrupt, speak for, or interpret what others are saying; no one is there to "help" or "tutor" others they perceive as "less" skilled or formally educated. At the end of each session, go around for "critique" or "self-critique."

- Design activities where the brilliance of everyone can shine. When the group is building its collective knowledge base, seek a wide range of experiences, data, and evidence. Surface lived experiences with the issue being studied, interview elders, excavate local knowledge and history, gather relevant music, and watch documentaries and pause at various points so people can jot down or speak their thoughts.

- Seek a diversity of perspectives and dig into disagreements. Be sure to have someone in the group tasked with asking, "Are there other thoughts? Does anyone have a different experience? What else is a possible response?"

- Break structured silences. Those of us who are academics, overeducated, or White often need to break structured silences so others feel free to raise contentious issues. A structured silence often surrounds topics that are taboo to raise, especially across power lines—age, race or ethnicity, gender, class. By openly recognizing that many of us live with privilege and others with the traumatic consequences of these structural dynamics, discursive windows open, and stigma can leave the space, freeing respondents to address conditions often constructed (and felt) as personal and/or shameful.

- Create an atmosphere where fear, love, trauma, anxiety, rage, or disappointment can be expressed. CPAR projects are typically focused on hot issues and traumatizing experiences, and when people who have endured these experiences are among the researchers, the experiences are a source of knowledge, a resource (not a bias). But they are in the room. Take time to assess what people need to be comfortable; what triggers, strategies, and ethics can be collectively developed to acknowledge that researchers on the team have different reactions to the topics being studied; and what different triggers and desires are needed for collective or self care.

In one study, Echoes of Brown, we were working with White, African American, Latinx, Asian American, and mixed-race students who were studying the experience of school integration and the unfulfilled promise of desegregation (Fine et al., 2004). The collective analyzed more than 12,000 student responses to a survey that included the question "Why are there such large racial disparities in college graduation?" One of our coresearchers was visibly upset as she read another student's response: "Because [ethnic group] are dumber than sh*t." The racism itself was not surprising, but reading it, as written, by someone her age, another student somewhere in the New Jersey/New York metropolitan area, struck a sobering chord. At that moment, we created a graffiti wall—a large piece of paper taped onto the wall, with headings that read "Most disturbing thing you have read," "Most exciting thing you have read," "Things you want to say back." At our end-of-day debriefs, we read from the graffiti wall, writing back to the original quotes, reflecting on feelings about the work, material, and ways we wanted to speak back.

Another example is messier: In one of our survey-building sessions for WYI, a small group of coresearchers was working in a room adjacent to the large space where most were gathered. As voices and laughter grew louder and more animated, I (MF) entered to ask the group to quiet down. My approach—too familiar, too glib, and far too intimate, particularly for a group less than 2 hours old—to asking them to "shush" was considered offensive by one of the activists. "Did you just enter a room full of queer youth of color and tell us to shut up?" The young person insisted that they call me out in public and suggested that I "be removed from the project." I had used my privilege badly, not thinking that my offhand attempt at "cute" humor would be read as aggressive, insulting, and frankly racist or homophobic and disrespectful. We spent a difficult hour working through the harm I had created and my reflections on how I misused privilege, and I offered an apology. That incident was a rough and very public and a crucial reminder that I—and White adults—must check our privilege and not assume intimacy or humor; I embodied and embody a long line of White authority figures who have misused their power before. The experience was difficult and, for me, transformative. If you are lucky, you will learn when you overstep, and you will take responsibility for harm and build the trust necessary for moving forward.

In your own CPAR projects, we hope that you will develop processes that invite coresearchers to bring their full selves into the research; handle dynamics of power delicately; hold space for difficult conversations; build corners where the pain, insult, joy, and pressures can be expressed; and invent processes for holding the group, as you journey together, in conversation about issues wounding, tender, and perhaps liberatory.

BUILDING AN ETHICAL RESEARCH COLLECTIVE: ETHICS AND INSTITUTIONAL REVIEW BOARDS

A word on ethics and the institutional review board (IRB) before we leave the design chapter: All research conducted through an academic institution must undergo an IRB review. As you have hopefully gathered by reading thus far, CPAR engages ethics far beyond what is asked by any IRB. In fact, we see CPAR as an ethical response-ability (Montgomery & bergman, 2017) to communities with whom we engage in research, and ethics is an ongoing process. In each CPAR project, we develop, collectively and through participation, a range of ethical frameworks that include, but go far beyond, "consent" and "anonymity" to consider, for example, respect, relationships, representation, compensation, naming (or anonymizing) people and organizations, language, vulnerabilities, and attributions. We recommend Guishard et al. (2018), Cahill et al. (2015), Sandwick et al. (2018), and the work of the wonderful Bronx Community Research Review Board (http://bxcrrb.org) for a rich consideration of ethics in community-based research.

To ground us, however, we offer a range of ethical questions that CPAR researchers should be discussing collectively. Most fundamental are the following:

- Respect. How do we honor the stories people share with us?

- Anonymity. What is anonymity "protecting"? IRBs typically require anonymity. However, in some contexts, this "protection" can feel patronizing. In others, it can reproduce exclusion, erasing people yet again from public discourse. In the Changing Minds study, most women, who already felt locked away, wanted to use their own names, to tell their stories for themselves. Talk with coresearchers and participants about whether (and how) people want to be anonymous or use names of their choosing.

- Vulnerability. Can we protect information that people have shared with us that may be used against them (e.g., if they are under surveillance, undocumented, living with an order of protection, vulnerable to lose their children)?

- Financial equity. How do we compensate people for their labor, their generous stories, and their travel and child care needs when they agree to participate in our projects (as researchers or even as interviewees)?

- Language. How are we describing ourselves and the people and communities with whom we are collaborating? Have we removed deficit, damaging, and condescending language? Are we using people-first language (e.g., people in prison, people with disabilities) and language generated by communities instead of language that reproduces disparaging or pathologizing frames (see the *Publication Manual of the American Psychological Association*; American Psychological Association, 2020)?

- Translation. Do we translate interviews conducted in a language other than English, and if so, do we retain some of the original spoken text?

- Grammar. Do we "clean up" grammar when using quotes from study participants? What if they ask us to?

- Accountabilities. Who will review our findings? Do other members from communities we are working with get to write a dissenting note or commentary? Do they get veto power over some of what the researchers have found or said?

- Authorship. How do coresearchers get authorship, credit, and funding?

- Writing and credit. Who will do the writing? Who will speak at policy gatherings? Who gets to represent the project? How will the academics challenge the typical assumptions that those connected to the university are the "real" researchers and everyone else is a "helper"?

- The narrative afterlife. What happens to the narratives after the project is over? Is it possible to store them in a local library archive as part of the ongoing history of the community or in the archive of the school, a prison-justice organization, an advocacy group, the Lesbian Herstory Archives, the Schomburg Library on African American History, El Centro for the history of Puerto Ricans in New York City?

Few of these questions arise in our formal university human subjects research ethics training or IRB applications—and yet they are critical to the integrity of a CPAR project.

CPAR REFLECTION

When engaged in policy work, it may be useful to generate or introduce already existing statistical evidence. If you do, (a) facilitate a participatory, community-based conversation to unpack "official statistics;" and (b) always, in addition, gather stories, experiences, and dreams of impacted people, groups, and communities. In building policy or theory, programs or social movements, we have found that designs that combine statistics with narratives are most compelling. This is not an argument against qualitative only studies; it is an argument for designs that center lives, groups, and communities represented in their full complexity.

3

PARTICIPATORY KNOWLEDGE PRODUCTION

Critical participatory action research (CPAR) adds a crucial "step" in the research journey, where members of the research team spend time together, sharing knowledge, speaking with critical informants and people who might be considered "outliers," and hosting tender discussions with a wide range of people before the "official" data collection commences. In the What's Your Issue? (WYI) project, this involved retreats and conversations among the 45 coresearchers and in our piloting sites across the country: exchanging struggles and joys, listening for counterstories, and recounting moments of structural and intimate violence and strategies for survivance (Vizenor, 1999). It also involved being attentive to unusual experiences, often discarded as "outliers" but treasured in CPAR; determining language and ethical commitments that were accessible, affirming, representative, and authentic to our experiences and, even more intimidating, for the survey that was about to float into the cyberworld; and searching for narratives—in our sampling strategies and the questions we pose—that would typically be hidden or dismissed in the shadows, under the covers, or in silence (Cammarota & Fine, 2008).

https://doi.org/10.1037/0000241-003
Essentials of Critical Participatory Action Research, by M. Fine and M. E. Torre

In this chapter, we explore how we produced knowledge collaboratively to fill in and enflesh the design we set out in Chapter 2. As you might recall, María and a smaller team of youth colleagues held phone interviews and assembled a stunning research collective to include 40 young people from Boston, Seattle, Mississippi, Detroit, New Jersey, New York, Tucson, St. Louis, Los Angeles, and New Orleans in New York for a series of three research meetings, for 3 days each, to engage in cross-national dialogues about lives, institutions, and activisms and create the study design and the survey, analyze the data, and think about results, actions, and design products. Unlike the Changing Minds study, where we had no budget, or FOSTERing Growth, with minimal funds to pay our coresearchers, WYI was well funded by a private philanthropy group, allowing us to finance travel, hotels, and food; pay research stipends for all coresearchers; and give each community project small grants to support local campaigns. To make participation as accessible as possible, CPAR projects should subsidize food, travel, child care, and labor as acts of respect, dignity, and care within the research process.

While the overarching design of the research was determined by the funder's desire for a national survey, we embarked on processes of collective knowledge building so that we could create a truly provocative survey that would fully invite and capture the vibrant, intersectional selves and experiences of respondents without throwing shade or disrespect. After several rounds and elaborate feedback from each, we decided to host a final—in-person—survey-making party to pilot the latest draft of the survey in New York City.

PILOTING: ACCOUNTABILITY TO AND FEEDBACK FROM THE COMMUNITY

We put out a call for LGBTQ+ and gender-expansive young people 14 to 24 to pilot the survey at a deli on a Saturday. We expected no more than 40 to attend. As it turned out, more than 150 young people streamed in, climbing the steps to the second floor. Friends had texted friends to come to a "social justice research project," where they could earn $15/hour for 4 hours for sharing their thoughts and opinions about what we referred to as a "bad draft" of the WYI survey, again attempting to signal that everyone participating had full authority to edit, revise, and rebuild it. Some youth brought their mothers; many more brought friends. Roy, a queer African American high school student, remarked, "I have never been with so many people like me without going through a metal detector." See Figure 3.1 for an image of the space we created for the beginning of our inquiry.

FIGURE 3.1. Youth Researchers Debating, Reviewing, and Critiquing Our "Bad Draft" of the Survey

Over lunch and laughter, we traded pronouns, pseudonyms, and real names and created and presented to the packed room crews' colorful banners that depicted "what the world should know about LGBTQ+ and gender non-conforming (which we later changed to gender-expansive) youth." We then split off into groups to critique, edit, revise, and remix the survey. Across rooms, groups, and arguments, we rewrote, added, and reassembled what would eventually become the final draft of the online survey of, by, and for LGBTQIA+ and gender-expansive youth, generated by young people, dedicated to lifting up not only the struggles of LGBTQIA+ and gender-expansive youth but also their intersectionality, creativity, passions, and ideas for political change.

In the room, the majority was youth of color with substantial wisdom-producing experience of being homeless, being pushed out of school, being aggressively policed, and negotiating alternative economies. There was a palpable excitement in finalizing a survey that was dedicated to representing the vast array of LGBTQIA+ and gender-expansive experiences while reaching out to and representing youth too often left out, written off as "too hard to reach." With this spirit, intense conversations grew as the group fleshed out the survey with standardized and homegrown questions about activisms and creativities, betrayals and worries, intersections and anxieties, gifts and dreams, floating questions such as "What would your ideal life look like?" "Where do you hope to be in 10 years?" "What do you need now?"

In one small room, 20 young people from various agencies, activist organizations, and educational settings met to discuss some of the more "contentious issues"—questions on pain, betrayal, and needs, questions that could produce data that, if misused, could lead to pathologizing peers. Long, difficult conversations ensued and were brought back to the larger group without consensus. Instead, "lively" debate ensued about what to include, how to phrase questions, what to ask, and what not to ask.

In no time, we were entering a dense conversation about terms and language, a moment that later helped us recognize the usefulness of CPAR in ensuring what we call *critical construct validity*. Our youth colleagues were having complex conversations about words, categories, and binaries psychologists rely on without thinking and then legitimate on surveys: Are you male or female? Homeless? Lesbian? Do you have psychological stress? Have you experienced domestic violence? As if we all agree on their meanings. But by looking at the rough draft of the survey collectively and with critical eyes, youth started questioning aloud, "How do I answer this?" "What's a woman?" "Is a trans man a man?" "What counts as family?" "If I live on my cousin's couch, am I homeless?" "Do police really protect?" "Am I lonely if I spend 8 hours online?" "Should a White-passing person of color really be classified as 'of color'?" "Is asexual a sexual orientation?" "If I don't get harassed by police because I am scared to go outside as an undocumented person, does that mean I have a lot of stress about police or none?" "If I am an online blogger, does that count as activism?" "If I feel most comfortable among trans women of color in social media sites, can I say that's where I find community?" These rich and complicated discussions revealed the power of CPAR dialogues and the limits of a survey, where words sit on a page and then fly out with little context or explanation into the virtual world, as if we all come to them with the same experiences, histories, and interpretations.

CPAR REFLECTION

Deep, participatory dialogue among widely diverse community members opens up important and sometimes delicate conversations for theorizing, design, methods, and analysis. Taken-for-granted constructs are questioned and thought through. It is in this phase that we engage critical construct validity.

Our youth colleagues were determined to contest the assumptions behind gender, sexuality, and identity, challenging binaries and fantasy that gender is stable. They further wanted us to know that gender and sexuality were only some of their important identities. This discussion led to a collective decision to open the survey with an opportunity for participants to name their intersectional identities in their own words, without pigeonholing them. In large part, because of this discussion, the survey opens with "What five words or phrases would you use to describe yourself?" which proved to generate incredibly rich information about how young people see themselves—and want others to see them. These open-ended invitations to introduce oneself in full complexity soon emerged as a sacred commitment of CPAR.

We display in Figure 3.2 a word cloud of the full sample—"five words"—drawn from our final sample of close to 6,000. The size of the words reflects how frequently the terms were used. We learned much about how LGBTQIA+ and gender-expansive young people describe themselves when given an opportunity for self-expression beyond the narrow confines of preexisting categories.

Like the opening question about "five words," the young people in the deli were insistent that we create space in the survey for respondents to describe in their own words their gender, sexuality, and race or ethnicity before asking them to check boxes. In response, we designed the survey so

FIGURE 3.2. A Word Cloud Representing LGBTQIA+ Youth Responses to "What Five Words Would You Use to Describe Yourself?"

that gender, sexuality, and race or ethnicity are explored in at least three ways, and here, order matters.

First, we offered open-ended questions—for example, "How would you describe your gender?" Then, we asked a closed-ended item with lots of options:

If you had to use the following categories, which best describe(s) your gender? (Check ALL that apply.)

❑ Woman   ❑ Genderqueer
❑ Man   ❑ Gender nonconforming (GNC)
❑ Trans man   ❑ Two spirit
❑ Trans woman   ❑ Questioning

And then, "If you feel like the question above does not represent your gender expression, please explain." We got a wide range of responses. Here are just a few:

Genderfluid

I don't have a perfect word for it, but I guess I'd say masculine-of-center woman

Amazing

I feel like I just exist

I feel definitively not male, but I don't care to be female either. I've always felt like I just "exist"

I am myself and nothing more

No thanks (agender)

Trans man publically [*sic*], gender fluid nonbinary personally

what gender? i don't have a gender, stop trying to label me with meaningless things 00*shrug emoji* Somewhere in the Agender/Demiflux zone

A work in progress, but currently seems trans-masculine

Everything at once, but also changing

HELLA CONFUSING

¯_(ツ)_/¯

We offer this small sampling simply to demonstrate that when you give people a chance to self-express, they are creative and unique. By doing this, we as researchers learn much about complex, dynamic, expressive subjectivities that conventional psychological studies have failed to capture with our boxes, even when we say "check all that apply."

FINALIZING THE INSTRUMENT: A QUALITATIVE PARTICIPATORY NATIONAL SURVEY?

After this last "survey-making party" pilot, we finalized the survey with our 40 core coresearchers from across the country. Ours was a highly unusual project: to develop with teens and young adults a qualitatively oriented, participatory national survey that blended "youth-produced" items submitted from around the country with traditional standardized measures, images, posters, open-ended questions, and an expansive call to respondents for "what else would you want to ask LGBTQIA+ young people?"

To attract a sample that was geographically diverse (including every other form of diversity), we produced a short #WHATSYOURISSUE? video that was shared via social networks and lived on our project website (https://www.whatsyourissue.org), where youth could learn about the project and take the survey. We hired a small team of queer youth of color fluent in social media to share the website and recruit respondents from across the nation. Please take a moment to watch it (https://player.vimeo.com/video/131826967).

Once the survey and website went "live," we monitored the demographics so that White respondents did not flood the sample, and we amplified strategic social media posts to assure racial and regional representation. While the sample grew, we collaboratively planned for research retreats that would focus on analysis and products and actions to share and animate the findings. The funding was distributed to LGBTQIA+ organizations and youth as our coresearchers, social media consultants, graphic designers, videographers, and of course, our survey participants.

CASCADING RESEARCH QUESTIONS: EVOLVING INQUIRIES IN THE PARTICIPATORY CONTACT ZONE

As in Changing Minds, the WYI research collective initially sketched out three straightforward areas for inquiry:

- Identities, desires, and struggles. What are the identities, desires, and struggles of an expansive national sample of LGBTQIA+ young people? (See Frost et al., 2019; Torre et al., 2018.)

- Confrontations with institutions of public life. How do race or ethnicity and geography intersect with gender and sexuality as young people negotiate relations with families, as well as police, schools, homeless shelters, child protective services, foster care, and the criminal punishment system? (See Frost et al., 2019.)

- Activism and solidarities. What forms of activism do queer youth engage in, and what kinds of intersectional solidarities do they pursue? (See Fine, 2017.)

Over time, however, as the research collective became an intergenerational think tank and as data poured in, stories unfolded, political conditions shifted in home communities, and new questions emerged nationally from the federal government. Thus, for instance, a major area of dispute concerned whether labels or categories "fit" on the bodies of LGBTQIA+ youth and gender-expansive youth. Queer young people were at the forefront of a generational move away from narrow definitions of identity, and we had an opportunity to understand this from within intergenerational participatory research. A short story of our experience will allow you to see how this tension about identity, categories, and binaries emerged as a core part of our inquiry, evoked only because we were a participatory, intergenerational research team.

Challenging Binaries and Categorizations

Once we were satisfied that we had a sufficiently vast, regionally representative, and racially diverse database, and given that we were all committed to intersectional analyses, it seemed obvious that we needed to disaggregate the full quantitative sample and compare respondents by race, gender, and sexuality to assess relations with police, schools, housing insecurity, and so forth. In a hugely naive and probably arrogant way, we (those based in the academy) announced that we were about to code the rich, open-ended self-descriptors into quantifiable categories of race or ethnicity, gender, and sexuality to conduct statistical comparisons and analysis. With analyses projected on the wall, the room collectively examined preliminary differences on negative contact with police for White respondents and respondents of color. The differences were, of course, striking. And so too was the outrage.

While the desire to showcase these differences was strongly shared, many of our coresearchers felt betrayed by the suggestion that WYI would shove respondents back into demographic boxes that we invited them to transgress in the open-ended question "Who are you?" Surprised and then infuriated, they made it clear that they fundamentally and unapologetically reject categories and labels that, at best, feel inadequate and, at worst, reproduce oppressive binaries. After much debate, our collective decided we would disaggregate the data for strategic use to show patterns of discrimination but that we would also produce videos from our qualitative interviews that would demonstrate the rich complexity of identities shared by youth participants, to be shared alongside the disaggregated data. Please take a moment to watch these videos (https://www.youtube.com/watch?v=veGAqxq9T5g; see also Short Docs Web Series, What's Your Issue, from CUNY TV: https://www.youtube.com/watch?v=DJGJ6gcxHzc).

From the clash and conversation that followed, a further research question was born. It was clear that we had to explore, drawing from both our discussions and the survey data, how LGBTQIA+ young people feel about the identities and categories that have been imposed on them and how they describe themselves with a bold sense of self-determination outside these categories.

Affirming Schools

At the second retreat, we opened space for an honest discussion of schooling. Most complained about alienation, bullying, and marginalization, and then D'Mitri, our coresearcher from Boston who identifies as he, she, they, spoke about the joy of attending a mostly Black, gay-affirming high school. D'Mitri detailed the core elements, and we realized we could "test" whether attending such a school bore positive academic and/or psychological outcomes. We decided to study the academic and mental health consequences of attending a dignity school (LGBTQIA+ affirming) compared with those of a nonaffirming school. This became a larger series of substudies on education and bullying documenting why "out" teachers matter; the importance of an LGBTQIA+ affirming curriculum in Language Arts, Sex Education, and History; and the impact of Gay–Straight Alliances and Gender-Sexuality Alliances on students' sense of belonging (Fine et al., in press).

The Cumulative Adverse Consequences of Housing Precarity for LGBTQIA+ Youth

At that same retreat, as we were reviewing the preliminary data from the first 3,600 respondents, we were running analyses in the moment, what Brett Stoudt (2014) called "stats-n-action," for questions posed by coresearchers. Lundyn, one of our coresearchers from New Orleans, suggested, "Let's look at how being homeless between 14 and 17 affects you after that." The data were stunning and devastating. We looked at the impact of housing precarity in terms of school dropout, negative contact with police, mental health concerns, economic troubles, and incarceration. For a small group, early homelessness was related to selling one's body for money, shelter, or drugs. Across racial and ethnic and gender and sexuality groups, homelessness proved to be a key adverse life event that affects disproportionately LGBTQIA+ and gender-expansive youth, with negative consequences snowballing over time. And so, we decided to investigate how housing precarity—being thrown out of one's parents' house or running away—affects academic, economic, and criminal justice outcomes by gender, sexuality, and region (Torre et al., 2018).

Activism as Survival and Resistance

As our conversations focused on sites of oppression by family, religious institutions, health care providers, social workers, foster care, police, prisons, and schools, some of the coresearchers reminded us that we also needed to document how queer teens and young adults resist, accommodate, survive, offer mutual aid, knit together chosen families, create healing spaces, and build safe-ish nests in dangerous worlds. And so, we decided to investigate: What are the creative coping and care work strategies LGBTQIA+ young people engage in? What strategies of resistance, healing, activisms, and solidarities do they pursue? (Fine et al., 2018a, 2018b; Frost et al., 2019; Torre et al., 2018).

Love Letter to Young People Who Identify as Neuroqueer

Most recently, Austin Oswald, working in solidarity with the project, has excavated the full qualitative database to lift out those young people who identify as "neuroqueer" because we noticed a substantial minority (close to 25%) of the self-descriptors were associated with mental health, psychiatric, and neurodiverse identities. Austin and Shéár Avory teamed up, both sharing life experiences with this group of participants, to write an essay on the identities, dreams, struggles, and desires of young people who identify as neuroqueer to educate, challenge, and provoke those in the mental health professions (Oswald et al., in press).

We elaborate this cascading of questions to reveal how complex and novel analyses and questions can emerge in critical dialogue.

GROWING A SAMPLE OF RADICAL INCLUSIVITY AND STRUCTURAL INTERSECTIONALITY

Throughout the months of data collection, we were monitoring the emergent demographics of the sample. Early on, we noticed that the survey sample was filling up with too many Whites, too many from the coasts, not enough from Alaska or Hawaii, not enough immigrants, few from the South, and so forth. With the strategic brilliance of our social media consultants and support of organizations and networks across the country, Twitter, and Tumblr, over 10,000 youth took the survey, but we committed to a conservative final sample of 6,073 young people who filled out 80% of the survey, from every state in the nation, Puerto Rico, and Guam. Our 6,073 succeeded in representing youth that had been too long ignored by the few national studies "on" LGBTQIA+ youth, providing stories of and by youth living lives at the structural margins and embodying a range of rich and complex intersectionalities. In the sample,

- 57% identified as trans, nonbinary, and gender expansive;
- 39% identified as youth of color;
- 23% described themselves as religious (Protestant, Roman Catholic, Hindu, Mormon, Jewish, Muslim, and Buddhist);
- 34% reported a disability;
- 48% were in middle or high school;
- 32% were currently in college; and
- 43% were in a relationship with a "special someone."

The final survey included three kinds of responses:

- standardized quantitative items that focused on health, mental health, depression, suicide, activisms, school belonging, family relationships, and stressors;

- open-ended lengthy narrative prompts, such as "Where do you find community?" "Describe your proudest moment" "How do you imagine your life when you are 25?" "What kinds of social movements are you involved with, and how?" "What questions would you like to ask other LGBTQIA+ young people?"; and

- open-ended short qualitative prompts, such as "What five words or phrases would you use to describe yourself?" or "If you were going to design a banner about yourself, what would it say?" "Describe your gender," "Describe your sexuality," and "Describe your race/ethnicity."

We were committed to honoring intersectionality, not squeezing complex persons into narrow demographic boxes, and amplifying the willful and wild subjectivities respondents offered us. Late in the survey, we presented an image of a banner and asked respondents to design a banner that reflected them. In the following, we offer a glimpse of gorgeous responses to the banner question (followed by self-described sexuality, gender, and race or ethnicity):

Womyn, queer, immigrant, Mexican. . . . How much more powerful could I get in this country? (Dykeness, cisgender, Mexican to the core, Maya/Aztec)

Just because I am a man with a vagina doesn't mean I can't be proud about it (Gay, male transman, caucasian)

I was born gay, were you born an asshole? (Natural, queer woman, White)

My PGP is PRISON ABOLITION (Queer, GNC butch, White)

I am #tamirrice I am #sandrabland I am #john crawford (Straight? nonbinary two-spirit GNC, Peruvian)

Disability is about a system of oppression, not about me being broken (Straight, transman, White)

Flexing my complexion over White supremacy (Gay, boy, multiracial Brazilian, Latino, Asian, Black)

Hug a Gay Mormon: We Exist!! (I am a boy who is attracted to other boys for emotional and physical reasons, I am Caucasian and my family stems from Europe. . . . I am LDS but have Jewish heritage and practice both Jewish and Christian holidays, White)

How am I still here? (Blackity Black, I'm Black y'all and Afrolatinx)

INQUIRY MARINATING IN COMMUNITIES OF CARE, CONCERN, AND ACTION

A beautiful aspect of CPAR is that the research design, types of questions posed, analysis, and the writing take form within a vibrant and eager community of interest, percolating with divergent perspectives, stitched together with a fair amount of trust, and committed to integrating empirical material from statistics, narratives, conversations, and radical (or hilarious) one-liners. This is the long arc of knowledge production, building mirrors and windows. We turn now to the delicate praxis of participatory analysis: aiming for material to be valid, accessible, provocative, and "of use."

4 PARTICIPATORY ANALYSIS
MOVING TOWARD ACTION

Participatory analysis attends to questions of dignity, intersectionality, and self-determination, respecting the language that respondents choose to use, and commits to moving the research toward action. As we have discussed so often, critical participatory action research (CPAR) builds research questions, designs, methods, and samples informed by the wisdom of a wide range of perspectives. That is true in the analysis as well. Without the pressure to agree but to learn with and from each other, in CPAR projects, we spend much time hearing everyone's interpretations, trying to understand where we overlap and where we differ and what new wisdom, visions, or questions might be borne from our rich dialogues of interpretation. Participatory analysis requires a strategy for systematic analysis within each form of data, and then weaving interpretations across the various methods—for instance, narratives and statistics. In this chapter, we walk through our process of participatory data analysis, anchored specifically in the What's Your Issue? (WYI) narratives that address "schooling" and "activism." We specify how we drew the sample, determined the narratives to read, generated codes, and appreciated "outliers" as whisperers from the margins telling us something quite special.

https://doi.org/10.1037/0000241-004
Essentials of Critical Participatory Action Research, by M. Fine and M. E. Torre

SLICING THE DATA

The quantitative and qualitative responses submitted by almost 6,000 respondents constitute a single WYI database. At any point that a new analysis is needed—when we were asked for an evidence-based amicus brief for a civil lawsuit on gender-neutral bathrooms in Tennessee or for expert opinion on a criminal lawsuit surrounding a murder associated with sustained homophobic bullying in a school in the Bronx or for a love letter to young people who consider themselves neuroqueer—we have been able to "select" a subsample of respondents and analyze with specificity their statistical and narrative responses. For instance, we can pull out of all respondents from the Southeast those who self-identify as undocumented or intersex or as trans women of color. We could create a subsample of all respondents who mention "activism" or "violence" across questions or those who left school before high school graduation.

This capacity to pull out subsamples is important for our solidarity work with a range of social movements. For instance, we were recently contacted by the director of a Native American college student program, asking whether we could send him the responses on "school," "proudest moment," and the "five-word" self-descriptors from the young people who identify as Native or Indigenous or with tribal affiliations. We sent him a word cloud, narratives on "proudest moment," and schooling stories that he has used within his community and foundation to build support for intersectional solidarities within and to fundraise for Native college students. This single-site database, blending demographic, quantitative, and qualitative materials, has proved to be comprehensive and flexible as we pursued various streams of analysis over time in support of varied communities and struggles, school districts, and youth groups.

In this section, we focus step by step on how we analyzed a sample of narratives that describe stories of schooling, so readers can see not only what respondents shared but also, more important, how we engaged participatory analysis: the phases of analysis, the decisions we made, and on a more granular level, how we created tight analytic codes for further interpretation.

STEPS OF PARTICIPATORY ANALYSIS: CULLING THE DATABASE, MACRO REVIEW, AND THEN CODING

We started with one question: "Please tell us a story about your proudest or happiest moment." Almost all (5,862) of our sample answered this question, and more than a quarter shared narratives (1,623) that could be categorized as "schooling stories." We read 20% of these stories (327)—every fifth—and coded for themes, surprises, and outliers.

Culling the Narrative Sample

At first, we, along with Allison Cabana (a research associate and doctoral student working with the collective), searched the full narrative database for stories of schooling. We decided to focus on "proudest moment," and we selected and pulled out all qualitative responses that included key words related to school. The key words were generated with coresearchers and included school, education, teachers, bullying, push out, drop out, GED, learning, student, and mentors.

CPAR REFLECTION

Just figuring out the keywords among a diverse group is theoretically delicate and conceptually rich. A notion as seemingly straightforward as "school stories" may evoke experiences quite distinct by race, gender, sexuality, and region and thereby stretch the range of search terms.

Participatory Reading Across Texts

Once the keywords were established and the 327 cases identified, we printed out all the narratives for the research collective to read. We met in small groups, read the narratives, underlined words we loved or did not understand, wrote notes in the margins, circled meaningful phrases, added question marks, jotted down our feelings in response to the narratives, and held small group discussions, and then in a larger full-group discussion, we shared our reactions, emotions, provocations, and what we learned. In this phase of *participatory reading across texts,* before we could even think about systematically coding the responses, we wanted to hear from the broad range of researchers and from our various perspectives ideas about codes, narratives that surprised us, common stories, and also outliers. We identified macro codes, including achievement and creative performance; surprises, including the frequency of "revenge" stories and a school nurse who snuck in LGBTQIA+ affirming videos; and outliers that seemed unpredictable and worthy of exploration: "I was proudest when I got my GED and my mother let me drop out!"

CPAR REFLECTION

Regardless of the topic, it is important to read through a diverse sample of all the narratives as a preliminary step before coding and host a session for the full research team to be able to read through the narratives and share perspectives, questions, and interpretations. Make sure the sample you are reading is diverse by key elements (not just the first submitted, or from one region or one racial or ethnic group).

Lifting Up Codes, Surprises, and Outliers

Reading across narratives, we heard stories of bullying, graduation, family rejection and embrace, peer harassment, academic success, getting into college, getting an A, and psychological distress. We read sweet stories of "victory" and recognition; that kiss in the bathroom; the teacher who apologized; the mother who said, with tears, "So, what's your preferred pronoun?"; a perfect performance in the marching band; and graduating from SUNY as a Black, multiracial, queer femme.

Across the full narrative subsample, we heard much about families, much about mothers, and little about fathers. We met teachers who changed lives: one who said "you won't bully anymore" to a homophobic peer and another "who was homophobic but I talked to her about my suicide and she became an amazing advocate for queer youth." We read about band leaders, Latin teachers, writing coaches, and mentors who encouraged and sometimes abused. We read revenge and exit stories: "I finally graduated and could leave high school behind," "I got a GED and my mother let me drop out!" "I finished high school online and was FREE!"

A significant cadre of young people submitted stories about the courage to exit—from abusive homes, violent relationships, oppressive schools, tortured contexts—marking their proudest moment. We all took a breath. Some codes could be found across the various submissions, such as homophobic kids at school, bullying, a loving parent, and a gay teacher who understood. But surprises and outliers were our treasured narratives, held to the side, with care.

This collective conversation among our broad research collective was infused with the statistical data on schooling that confirmed the experiences of many of our coresearchers: substantial levels of school-based alienation, suspensions or disciplinary charges, and bullying, particularly for LGBTQIA+ young people of color and most particularly for those living in the southern states. Many of the stories we read described academic pain, alienation, bullying, and feeling alone and closeted. But we have learned that as soon as it feels like a consensus is settling in, to wait a beat. It is important in CPAR to hold space for the counterstory.

We were discussing high school, and there were echoes of feeling "like I don't belong." Then D'mitri, a coresearcher from Boston, raised a hand and told us about their high school experience at the Boston Arts Academy: "My school was full of out gay teachers, African American teachers. I felt loved and liberated." Once this counterstory was introduced, others contributed stories of educational joy, desire, and engagement. The youth researchers from St. Louis, we discovered, were working on an LGBTQIA+ affirming sex education course, as were the researchers from Boston working with a community-based organization. Two researchers from Jackson, Mississippi, were collaborating with African American students in a statewide network organizing for Mississippi chapters of the Gay–Straight Alliance, but teachers in Mississippi were fearful they would lose their jobs if they were the sponsors. The thick and complex layers of schooling—pain, desire, joy, accomplishment, resistance—were revealing themselves.

In reading the narratives together, we decided to read aloud a few outliers and get people's interpretations. Someone read, "Once I came out, some of the boys who bullied me congratulated me; told me they liked my talk; they applauded my spoken word." The discussion unraveled a complex dynamic that most—but not all—the youth researchers recognized. When a young person is in the closet, the bully has a weapon: the secret. But once the student comes out, the weapon becomes lame; they are no longer vulnerable.

CPAR REFLECTION

Take time to read and listen carefully to outliers. Read the marginalia on surveys. Someone took the time to convey these unusual tidbits. They may be just that: an unusual story. Or, more likely, these respondents are telling a story that many could but few dare to speak. Outliers have so much to teach us (see Stoudt, 2016).

Another set of participants offered up stories of joyous self-determination and self-expression, often following an experience where they were misread, disrespected, or so constrained that they could not express their full selves. We read aloud about the pleasure of other people using "my preferred pronouns and preferred names" and pride in one's self-described gender, sexuality, and disability, written in cursive and Latin, showing off my "bad ass curves" in high heels and a male Reserve Officers' Training Corps (ROTC) uniform.

> **CPAR REFLECTION**
>
> Wait for or search for stories of joy, resistance, and creative survival sitting just behind, beneath, or after events of betrayal, abuse, neglect, and marginalization—you will find them.

CODING: THE STORIES AND ANALYSIS

Once we exhausted our analysis of codes, surprises, and outliers, we decided to work with the 327 narratives and develop codes for the full narrative. With a diverse sample, we simply pulled out every fifth response to "What is your proudest moment?" and coded, on an Excel spreadsheet, responses with multiple codes—for instance, academic achievement and relationships or activism and creative performance. We piloted for interrater reliability on the codes (two people read each narrative and tried to come to 80% agreement on their coding). This version of reliability is rarely a practice of CPAR. After that, each narrative was coded by a single person.

In thinking about your experience with analysis and coding, there are a series of CPAR coding decisions that research teams might consider:

- Can the full group read through all the narratives or a diverse subsample for identifying macro themes, surprises, and outliers?

- Who will generate the working list of keywords and then codes?

- How will you determine the sample of narratives to read to generate codes and establish them? These are hard decisions, but please be sure the sample of texts you review are from a diverse sample of respondents.

- What unit will be coded (word, sentence, paragraph, full narrative)?

- Do you care about interrater reliabilities and how many people will be involved in establishing them?

- How will evocative outliers be represented and not lost in the analysis and writing?

- How will intersectionality and rich contradictions be folded into the coding process?

- Can narratives be coded for multiple themes?

- How will the final write-up represent the qualitative material? By presenting a life? A theme with quotes from many? An outlier? Will the narratives be woven in with the quantitative data (in a mixed-methods project) or presented separately?

- How will confidentiality of the narratives be assured if the respondent names a school, person, or an incident?

- How will structures, policies, ideologies, and institutional dynamics be made visible as they shape and are shaped by persons who offered up the narratives? (For instance, if a student feels "alone" in a school, and there is a policy that LGBTQIA+ teachers cannot be out in school, is the feeling of being alone not just intrapsychic but actually a dynamic between institutional policy and how a young person walks through the school?)

In any qualitative project, but particularly CPAR, we highly recommend that a diverse group read all (or a sample of) the narratives and only then move into the more—but sometimes flattening—process of placing the narratives into coding categories. You may decide to use a computer program (e.g., Atlas.ti, Dedoose, Nudist) to organize the material, but these are filing systems that can never replace the analytical work you do with your coresearchers. Programs can pull and organize words or phrases out of a larger narrative and then clump them with others' words and phrases that sound alike, but too often context is lost, as is meaning, sarcasm, irony, emotions, and nuance.

While coding is, of course, considered necessary to theorize themes and dynamics that cut across a sample, we know from years of doing this work— especially when working with youth—coresearchers are often not happy about stuffing a complex, multilayered narrative into a single dimension code. Coding can feel like a way of "making sense" of a pile of narratives, or it can feel like a dissection of a complex text, a distortion of the original intentions of the writer, and perhaps even a methodological betrayal of the respondents. And yet, after much fruitful discussion, code we did.

CREATING A CODEBOOK

After multiple conversations, we finalized a list of seven codes in two buckets: Contexts of pride (academic achievement, creative performance, activism) and social–psychological dynamics of pride (relationships, coming out, recognition, mental health struggles). After reading the material, it was clear that respondents were telling us about pride in context (where or what they felt pride in) and relationships (with whom and how).

We did not expect so many would introduce creative performance, activism, or mental health struggles. Nor did we anticipate that the relational dynamics that enable pride or happiness would be central to the stories shared. In retrospect, of course, it all makes sense. A vibrant group of young people, seeking and being denied recognition, might well nest prideful moments within an experience of being seen and re-cognized. We just did not know that before. Or at least, the traditionally trained researchers, who had read all the literature, did not anticipate how often revenge, recognition, and "getting out of here" would emerge as "proudest moments."

Most stories of schooling were coded as narratives of academic achievement (90), discussing graduation or SATs, passing Latin, or learning to write cursive. Often, they were described as a victory, despite the odds. A number crafted revenge stories about proving oneself to teachers, family, and peers who did not believe; finding the courage to give a paper about anxiety or sexuality; or deciding with glee to leave high school and get a GED. Many of these are simply and beautifully young people's stories. But in these stories, young people narrate academic achievements as survivors, surviving as an outcast, surviving on one's own terms, surviving despite the odds, and surviving with an attitude (and doing splits):

> On my high school graduation day when the school called out my birth given name but my friends and the crowd cheered my preferred name.

> WHEN i graduated from high school i was the only few gays kids at my school and i had come out of foster care and was living on my own rite before i graduated so i said in class to a friend that i was going to do the splits on stage at graduation . . . and i did i was so proud i had made it because those 4 years of my life were very tumultuous.

> I stood up in front of my entire psychology class and gave a presentation on social anxiety disorder, which I am diagnosed with. When I was finally finished, I received a HUGE round of applause from the entire class, and it felt so, SO good. I had done it! And I'm still so proud of that, to this very day.

We hear pride in achieving and overcoming and a focus on gender and sexuality and anxiety. We hear justice in recognition, accomplishment, and applause.

The second most popular category included school-based stories of creative performance (69): theatre, marching band, orchestra, poetry slams, fashion shows, writing, sports, and anime. Performance spaces opened opportunities to meet "friends who accept me" and to "speak out for those who can't yet" and a chance to "change stereotypes" and "work against my social anxieties." These too are a blend of the familiar, the banal, and the daring:

> I won the poetry slam at my school when I was 19, a senior in high school. I slammed about queer issues, being closeted, feeling like I could never be who I wanted to be, etc. A lot of the other poets, many of whom my friends, were also queer, and I wanted to speak for those who weren't out yet and who couldn't speak about it. It was also an attempt to get my parents to understand what it felt like for me to be queer and to get people in general to understand, which I hope they did. I dunno, it was a really amazing time, slamming about something so important to me.

> I was participating in a queer fashion show that a group at my university put on every spring, which is essentially an incredible art showcase of self-expression. I was a part of a group cat-walking the stage in clothes made out of condoms, which was amazing! But at intermission, there was a group doing a "My Secret Fashion" finale at the end. So I got in a sports bra, comfy panties, high heels and painted "no you can't watch" with two connected female symbols on my back and walked that stage! I felt so proud to have the confidence to stand in front of hundreds of people in hardly any clothing, being my badass, feminist, curvy, sexy self!

Activism (51) was yet another lifeworld where young people expressed pride and happiness, where they developed, displayed, and were encouraged to express a more grounded sense of self and collective purpose, taking leadership in a religious community, Gender and Sexuality Alliance, PRIDE, school council, or classroom. Some joined, and others built a community. Some expressed pleasure at "modeling" courage for others and hearing that "my struggle helped someone else."

> When I took a trip to Tulsa, OK, with my GSA group from a smaller town in Oklahoma and we attended the gay pride event. . . . I was able to lead young, queer high school kids from Oklahoma to shout "I'm queer and I'm here!" in the streets of busy downtown Tulsa. Most of these kids have faced verbal and physical harassment for their gender identities and sexual orientations so watching them be so carefree for a day was amazing.

> My proudest moment was protesting the transphobic bathroom bill that would reward students $2,500 for "finding other students in the wrong bathroom." I was in the closet about my gender identity . . . harassed in the bathroom because of my presentation. Our protest was even enough to garner a counter protest from the Westboro Baptist Church. Thankfully, our school was very supportive and replied with a fundraiser for the Kansas City Anti-Violence Project. Seeing that love made me feel less hesitant about coming out in the future.

Beyond where these young people experienced pride, we heard much about how, with whom, and why.

The desire to be recognized was poignant as an affective stream across the narratives—the thrill of being seen, known, named, and recognized in all one's complexity. This could happen in a quiet field or a crowded trans-solidarity rally in Tulsa, within the Latter-day Saints community or at my Quaker meeting, in science class or the boys' bathroom, or by dressing in an ROTC male uniform or wearing high heels. It was interesting to hear these stories about deeply unsafe spaces—ROTC or the Mormon church—reflecting incredible courage and joy.

> When I got the male's uniform for ROTC, I was with a couple of friends. I had the uniform at the beginning of the year, then it got taken away. . . . I met another trans guy; we talked a lot about him and his life at home and school. He told me I really needed to talk to my senior chief . . . 2 weeks later on uniform day, I was hanging out with some of my friends after school who are also in ROTC; we were waiting for practice to start and a senior came and told me I get to wear the guys uniform, so we went in the supply room and got it. It fit perfectly; I was so excited.

> The happiest moment I have had in my entire life was when I was 15 years old, and I finally decided that I was going to be 100% okay with who I am. Up until then I had felt so overwhelmingly conflicted constantly. I was raised in the LDS (Mormon) church, which treats religion like a cult lifestyle. Since day one I was constantly exposed to messages about what was "true" and "right." By the time I was a freshman I was attending church every single day but Saturdays. Thoughts of whether or not God would be okay with what I was doing dominated my life. . . . I knew more about . . . [the Church's version of] Christ than I did about myself. . . . I was always told that being anything other than cis and heterosexual was an abomination in God's sight. I fell into a depression. I felt like I was being torn into two pieces. As cliché as it sounds, it seemed like I had a constant, never-ending physical pain from the emotional torment. It got to the point where I simply could not take it anymore. I knew that if this continued, I would probably end up dead. So, about a month before I turned 16, I slipped out of the house while my family was watching sermons on the TV. I ran out to the very back of a huge field near our house, and I layed down and thought about everything—my church, my feelings, what thoughts and morals were truly my own versus what thoughts had been forced onto me by others, and I realized that I had my own life. It wasn't anyone else's, and I couldn't waste it on other people. I had no clue if a God really existed, but if one did and made me feel as horribly about myself as I had been feeling, then it wasn't a god who deserved my worship. I vowed then and there that I would learn to love myself the way I was, and as soon as I got my own life and moved away to college, I would live it how I wanted to, loving who I wanted to, and being who I wanted to be.

Reading these proudest moment narratives, we heard much about how deeply important and life sustaining relationships are to young people, particularly for those who have been betrayed, misunderstood, rejected, or abused by those most intimate to them. School stories were peppered with sweet (and sour) relations with friends, family (biological and chosen), peers, allies, and even former bullies.

It was the morning after I came out to my mom when I was 15. I was walking to school. Spring was just beginning, and as I walked, I felt the warmth of the sun on my skin and admired the blossoming trees and flowers surrounding me. I could hear the birds singing and the bees buzzing with happiness, and it almost felt as if they were all cheering for me. For the first time in my life, I felt liberated and entirely happy.

When I graduated from high school. I had this moment of "it's all over, and I didn't do a fucking thing," and then as I was leaving, I was hugged from behind by a friend of mine. They were crying their eyes out. They told me then that my struggle had given them the courage to explore their identity and realize they were also trans. That's when I realized I had actually done something good.

Within intimate relationships and sometimes in large auditoriums, coming out stories were deeply embedded in social contexts, with pride defined as feeling "incredible," "safe," and sometimes just hilarious.

Okay, this is going to sound really dumb, but it's the only time I've officially come out to someone, so I'm proud of it. Eighth grade, was in science class. Got a bendy ruler and said to my best friend, "This ruler is straighter than I am." And I just can't believe I said that.

And finally, we read a small but significant smattering of prideful stories about living with mental health struggles, enduring the oppressive weight of psychological struggles, anxieties, and depression and also the joy of over-coming, embracing, claiming, and building a queer community within psychiatric institutions, working on suicide hotlines, and engaging in conversations about gender and sexuality within autism camp.

When I was 16, I attempted suicide. My happiest moment was my 19th birth-day. I was at my top college with all of my friends, and we were at a college party. It was so beautiful because we were hanging out, dancing, having fun. And I couldn't help but smiling because they accept me and love me for who I am. And I am alive and loving life.

I can't remember my happiest moment. Because most moments are fleeting and saturate with other feelings and are vulnerable to retrospect and change. But I can tell you the time where I was most calm. It wasn't a big event or an adventure but more of just a moment where I collected myself and said I was happy. Well it's not THE best moment, but it's more eventful for me to talk about (most of my best moments are nothing to TALK about, they just 'were'). I was suffering from major depression and suicidal thoughts to the point where I attempted suicide and checked myself into a psychiatric ward during college (which was halfway across the nation from my family). I was so scared for while because I regretted it and want to go back so my grades won't slip and I wouldn't be near all these "crazy" people. But after a while, I learned more about mental illness and disabilities, and people there showed their kindness to me, no matter how different they were. They gave me extra blankets and snacks whenever and tried to give me their favorite cigarettes during smoke breaks. I met another gay college student who suffered from severe anxiety, and we talked for hours and found old *X-Files* episodes, which the nurses let us watch in the TV room. I felt like I was happy for the first time in months. I felt like my energy was replenished and going outside after the first time in 7 LONG days in a hallway made me appreciate my freedom to do anything.

We hope you have taken the time to read these narratives as gifts shared by the youth who took our survey. With such braided lives, spliced with ridicule and revenge, transgressions and silence, pain and laughter, it is indeed difficult if not unethical to simply "code" in ways that count up or even pull a part of a narrative out of a full life. In the chapter on writing, we explore these dilemmas with a bit more depth, but for now, we are glad you got to meet some of our 6,000 respondents.

Participatory analysis is the conceptual and empirical lifeblood of CPAR—novel ideas emerge among diverse researchers drawing on a mosaic of empirical material. And an imagination for action, policy, and transformation is lit. Old ideas are discarded, and new framings catalyze in evidence-rich dialogues among researchers who bring different biographies, standpoints, and lines of analysis to the work. Across narratives, we have tried to demonstrate how participatory analysis shifts and expands what we know about schooling and activism and reveals so much about what we have yet to learn.

BENDING ANALYSIS TOWARD ACTION

Martin Luther King Jr.'s declaration that "the arc of the moral universe is long, but it bends toward justice" has been held by many of us as we engage in long-term struggles. As we have argued throughout this small volume, CPAR projects are similarly designed to bend—in questions, design, method, and analysis—toward justice. Projects bend toward transformation, toward provoking shifts in consciousness and policy, through education or performance, in courtrooms, political campaigns, classrooms or community life, around kitchen tables or on social media, for audiences of impacted community members and (not yet critical) elites. Throughout the arc of CPAR projects, from the beginning through to the end, research teams consider who needs to hear the findings, where results should be circulated, and what forms of dissemination—scholarship, policy white papers, protest, legal action, performance, art exhibits, interactive archives—might be most compelling. How should the data be used to provoke and still protect those most vulnerable? How might the research activate change and not incite backlash?

Actions borne of CPAR are as diverse as theoretical frameworks, methods, and the composition of contact zones. In the case of the Changing Minds study, we sent the final report to governors in all 50 states and presented policy analysis to state legislatures, departments of corrections, universities, and organizing groups led by persons who were formerly incarcerated. The "report" included photographs and handwritten letters, as well as pull-out postcards with specific findings that readers could mail to legislators. The overall findings have been used by college admissions officers to "open" admissions to persons in prison and those just released. Other "actions" that resulted were found in the ripples of presentations. One happened early on, after sharing the research with children of women incarcerated at Bedford Hills Correctional Facility who then decided to produce a participatory documentary in their own voices—*Echoes of Incarceration*—by and for children impacted by incarceration (https://www.echoesofincarceration.org).

In the case of WYI, a range of actions continues to unfold. Soon after we completed data collection, Shéár Avory was hired by the Joseph Biden Foundation and brought disaggregated data by state, race and ethnicity, gender, and sexuality to the foundation to inform their programming. A few years later, there was a tragic murder at a high school in the Bronx, rising out of unaddressed homophobia in the school. We consolidated the WYI findings into an "expert report" for a lawsuit about bullying and homophobic school violence, ignored by school officials, ending with a peer-to-peer murder.

Opportunities for the WYI data to "be of use" have often been organic, arising after presentations of the findings, when audiences see entanglements between the data and their work and the communities of which they are a part. After once such presentation particularly about "dignity schools" at the New York City Board of Education, we joined forces with an amazing group called the Proud Educator Initiative, a vibrant and intersectional mobilization of queer educators in New York City fighting for the right to be their full selves in the classroom (https://www.proudteacherinitiatve.org). Pouring our data into their campaigns (e.g., our finding that LGBTQIA+ students report less depression, are less likely to consider dropping out, and are less likely to experience bullying when they attend schools with "out" educators; that all students benefit when educators can be their full, complex selves in the classroom), we have been collaborating on oral histories, videos, and documentaries by out educators and administrators about benefits for all. Another presentation of the findings to a coalition to end girls' incarceration led to creating products with the data to support decarceration of girls and meeting with a range of juvenile justice facilities to support queer justice before, during, and after incarceration.

Most recently, in the midst of COVID-19 and with deep concerns about people most vulnerable in prison, we have reconvened many members of our Changing Minds collective, who are now home, with lawyers and advocates who are mobilizing for the release of elderly or sick prisoners. We meet on Zoom and engage in "rapid response" CPAR, rooted in the wisdom of women now released, as we carve out legal and organizing strategies, research, and policy to reach those who remain behind bars and to pressure legislators for immediate action.

With humble reflection, the space between research and action is delicate and can at times be disappointing, littered with the well-worn obstacles of oppressive systems, resistance, and silencing (Zeller-Berkman et al., 2020). Researchers must do more than "disseminate" or publish findings. That said, those of us dedicated to publicly engaged scholarship confront the stark reality that injustice is, of course, not simply a cognitive problem. Data alone will not dismantle structural violence. And yet, the sweet and powerful solidarities sutured together in CPAR projects birth the joy of discovery, awaken us to the force of interdependence, make visible counterstories, lift up pain and laughter, and offer visions of different tomorrows, all of which works again and again to light the fuse of radical imagination. It is in this spirit that CPAR can become a cross-generational freedom dream, drawing from poets, activists, statisticians, artists, qualitative researchers, and community practitioners. While some research projects work on the "inside" of systems and others at the radical rim, they all, with the encouraging words of the poet Emily Dickinson, "Tell the truth, but tell it slant." This is the work of CPAR.

Other contemporary examples to prime the imagination include Regina Langhout, who has been gathering stories, collaborating with fourth graders, and painting murals to portray the violence of U.S. Immigration and Customs Enforcement in schools and universities (see Langhout & Vaccarino-Ruiz, 2020). Langhout, an activist scholar, recently issued a powerful policy statement for the Society for Community Research and Action, integrating all the evidence on the devastation wrought by deportation, family separation, and the local and national impacts of state surveillance of and violence on immigrant students, families, and communities (McNulty, 2019). Sharing similar commitments, Jennifer Ayala gathers with collectives of students, activists, and family and community members at The Center for Undocumented Students, which she directs at Saint Peter's University, to hold healing circles, collect oral histories, carve sanctuary space, catalog resistance strategies, and host advocacy seminars for, with, and alongside undocumented students, DACAmented students, and family members (see Ayala et al., 2020).

In another example, Madeline Fox and youth researchers in Brooklyn drew attention to a long-neglected underpass that serves as a vital pedestrian artery for entering their community in Red Hook, Brooklyn. Their research caught the attention of the Department of Transportation, and new walk light times were implemented (Fox, 2019). Although immediate changes are not always realized, CPAR has been effectively used to create processes for youth inquiry and legislative engagement, such as the legislative internship program of the Mestizo Arts & Activism Collective in Salt Lake City, Utah (see https://maacollective.org/projects/maali/).

All of these "actions"—grown at the intersection of research and action and amplified through art, scholarship, performance, litigation, protest, healing circles, community education—are essential to the praxis and heart of CPAR. Our point is simple: CPAR is both aspirational and accountable for action, change, and transformation, engaged through a wide range of strategies. This move from analysis to action is never straightforward, never simple, almost always fraught, and never enough. Participatory researchers must be engaged in collaboration, with a bold vision of evidence as a humble resource in struggles for justice, advanced through the voices, desires, lines of analysis, and dreams of those most impacted.

5 VIBRANT VARIATIONS AND GROUNDING QUESTIONS

We offer here a brief reflection on variations of critical participatory action research (CPAR) approaches. We invite you to consult the Public Science Project website (https://www.publicscienceproject.org) and our appendix to tour through a wild garden of projects, with examples of feminist PAR, street PAR, youth PAR (YPAR) in the classroom, PAR with people in prison, and PAR with labor organizations, projects rooted in critical statistics and engaged with participatory mapping. While there are differences across these variations in terms of who is part of the research collective (youth, people in prison, community members, college students), which methods are adopted or adapted (critical statistics, narratives, mapping, history), where the inquiry takes place (across transnational networks, in institutions, in schools, on the streets, online), or what kinds of final products, writing, and performances the collective creates, these variations within PAR are epistemic siblings—all are committed to the deep participation in all aspects of the research, to the extent possible, by those most impacted by injustice (see also https://www.yparhub.berkeley.edu).

Across these participatory genres, you will find a few shared nonnegotiables: Those most impacted and historically silenced must be centered as

https://doi.org/10.1037/0000241-005
Essentials of Critical Participatory Action Research, by M. Fine and M. E. Torre

architects of the inquiry, there must be ongoing critical analyses of power, and the research should be designed to facilitate some form of social change, in theory, policy, representations, and education through the arts, social movements, or public attitudes (see Ayala et al., 2018; Cahill, 2010; Fine et al., 2003; Fox, 2015; Galletta, 2013; Munoz-Proto, 2009; Payne, 2013; Stoudt et al., 2016). Beyond this, variations blossom, and subfields have a robust following.

YPAR is an extremely popular field within educational studies and psychology (see Caraballo et al., 2017; Giraldo-García & Galletta, 2015; jones et al., 2015; Kirshner & Pozzoboni, 2011; Langhout & Vaccarino-Ruiz, 2020; see also https://www.yparhub.berkeley.edu). Azzam et al. (2020) collaborated with teens in Cleveland who documented the closures of their schools, while Caitlin Cahill, David Quijada Cerecer, Matt Bradley, and youth researchers from the Mestizo Arts & Activism Collective (https://maacollective.org/) gathered oral histories from undocumented students mobilizing for educational access and against xenophobic attacks on their communities by organized militias and the state (Cahill et al., 2010). Street PAR, developed by Yasser Payne (2013), or Black PAR, advanced by Drame and Irby (2016), have a strong scholarly presence in sociology, critical psychology, urban education, and Black studies. Transnational PAR (see Ayala et al., 2020) and the transformative work on decolonizing methodologies (Land, 2015; Smith, 1999; Tuck & Yang, 2012) have been mobilized from Indigenous grounds and across national borders, addressing issues of land and language, racial capitalism and colonialism, sovereignty, and solidarities. Critical labor studies scholars have embraced CPAR, as illustrated by Do Lee (2018) and colleagues, working with bicycle food delivery workers situated at the nexus of labor and immigrant exploitation, and housing justice organizers in the United States (Billies, 2017) and Hungary (Udvarhelyi & Dosa, 2019), who have used CPAR as a strategy for advancing bold campaigns for housing with dignity.

Issues of intersectionality and structural exclusions have been investigated by research collectives such as Ronelle Carolissen and colleagues (2017) in South Africa, who have used participatory methods to unpack White South African resistance toward diversity; Karla Galvão (2015), working with teens and women in the Brazilian port town of Recife, who have blended sexuality education and participatory inquiry to address sexual violence and reproductive health when the oil industry brought thousands of men into their community; Mayida Zaal and colleagues, who have been collecting testimonies from educators who are "teaching while Muslim" (https://www.teachingwhilemuslim.org); and Cory Greene, who, with H.O.L.L.A. (How Our Lives Link Altogether; https://www.shorturl.at/cnLXZ), a youth-led intergenerational group in Brownsville, Brooklyn, uses CPAR as an organizing strategy to document, film, and create music as part of a national healing justice campaign. All of these projects center the wisdom (Freire, 1970; hooks, 1984; Horton, Kohl, & Kohl, 1997) of those most vulnerable and most daring and engage action as a praxis woven into inquiry.

Movement-based participatory research projects working with state governments confront a distinct set of challenges and opportunities. Sarah Zeller-Berkman engages CPAR and intergenerational policy making by activating youth councils, activism programs, advocacy organizations, and youth organizing as participatory designs in city governments (Zeller-Berkman et al., 2020). She and I (MET) have been collaborating with a progressive office of children's services in Florida, facilitating deeply participatory, painful, and raw dialogues between children removed from their homes, foster parents, biological parents, and social workers to address the harms inflicted and reimagine other practices to support and strengthen family relationships. In another example, Celina Su (2017) wove CPAR into the intersection of critical race theorizing and participatory budgeting processes. All three of these projects sit at the delicate membrane between participatory democracy and state government, building community power, widening the circle of key voices, and yet running into predictable obstructions (or cooptations) that happen within bureaucracies.

GROUNDING QUESTIONS FOR CRITICAL PARTICIPATORY INQUIRY

While we are all working in shared epistemological traditions and solidarities and—in widely different contexts—confronting similar forms of resistance and often quiet possible openings, there are a set of key questions that may help you anticipate the design details of your project:

- Who should be included as the members of the research collective? As we have stated, CPAR understands the space of the research collective to be that of a participatory contact zone. While many of the examples here stress bringing together "diverse" research collectives, some CPAR projects intentionally recruit a research team comprising only, or majority, impacted people (see *The People's Report*; Payne, 2013), all Black or Latinx people (see Drame & Irby, 2016), all undocumented people, or all people who identify as women and/or femmes. Who raises important considerations? There are no right answers, but there are important conversations to be held.

- To whom and for what are we accountable? Does the research team want to speak to the community and/or policy makers, the public, lawyers and advocates, or all these groups? Is the research designed to heal communities in pain, demand justice for structural inequities, or tell another story about how this community has survived and resisted? Does the project want to contribute to scholarship on the issue, a white paper on policy, or cartoons and zines? Will it make music or art from the narratives gathered, curate an art show, present oral histories in the local library, host an online archive of long-silenced stories, or craft an op-ed? Will the team make T-shirts, hold a local "sidewalk science" event, or present findings to the local teachers union or town council meetings?

- Can a project be "too inclusive" across lines of power? While we typically advocate for bold inclusivity, there are important conversations— and sometimes limits—about who should be part of the research team. In some contexts, power is rigidly hierarchical and potentially punitive, often meted out behind doors hermetically sealed off from accountability (e.g., in schools, prisons, the military, communities under surveillance). In such cases, the idea that "everyone is at the research table" is simply naive and potentially dangerous. In the Changing Minds project, we did not invite correction officials or the superintendent who held concentrated authority over the women into the research team (see Fine et al., 2003), though we did purposefully decide to interview them and others known to be critical of the college program. How wide the circle can be without collapsing from the weight of power inequity can only be determined locally, contextually, and in power-sensitive conversation.

- How will threats of state surveillance as well as community and individual vulnerability be navigated? Today, in times of heightened state surveillance (online and in person) and violence in communities of color, immigrant and Muslim communities, and some activist communities, there is a pronounced reluctance among many of those most impacted to participate in research projects for fear of exposure, retaliation, or deportation (see Stoudt et al., 2016, on the Morris Justice Project; Ayala et al., 2018, on PAR *EntreMundos*). Navigating power and vulnerability while maximizing meaningful participation requires delicate conversations. The issue is never whether those most marginalized are included but rather how we create the conditions for collaborating in solidarity and without increasing risk for people who have been targets of oppression.

- What forms of evidence should be collected? Research collectives must ask themselves, what is the purpose of the work? What forms of evidence will speak to desired audiences? Revisiting the question of to whom the research is accountable, teams must ask what they need from us and what we need to say. The decision to gather different forms of evidence through mixed methods is often made by CPAR collectives who wish to "speak back" to systemic abuse and also produce their often-overlooked or dismissed evidence. Morris Justice Project researchers in the South Bronx, for instance, wanted to systematically build an alternative community-generated database that could speak alongside the New York Police Department data on the use of "stop and frisk" (Stoudt et al., 2016). They surveyed community members in their 42-block neighborhood about their experiences with and attitudes toward the police. They then circulated the data within the neighborhood through street-corner "sidewalk science" installations and among lawyers and activists involved in lawsuits against the racially discriminatory use of stop and frisk in New York City.

At Montclair High School in New Jersey, 25 members of the Gender and Sexuality Alliance kept daily diaries for a week, tracking incidents of racism and homophobia experienced, overheard, or witnessed that were enacted by teachers and students—no names, just events were recorded. On Friday afternoon of the data collection week, they dumped all these incidents, keyed with day and hour and whether the incident was caused by a student or teacher, into a Google doc. After 2 months, they used their database to produce an extensive report, delivered to the school at a Montclair Education Association meeting. They also created a paper zine of comics incorporating their findings into a "welcome" to incoming first-year students, and they plastered the school's hallways with some of the offensive quotes in their data, scrawled on butcher-block paper, asking students as they walked by, How does this make you feel? The posters had open spaces inviting students to write back, in polyvocal streams of consciousness, to the discriminatory quotes. In these projects, communities took research into their own hands to speak back to those with power—police, peers, educators—with the hope of shifting culture and policy.

- At what scale? CPAR projects are hatched across a range of scales. They can be hyperlocal, as in the South Bronx neighborhood and Montclair High School. They can be translocal, as in the What's Your Issue? study (Torre et al., 2018). They can be institutional, as in the Changing Minds study at Bedford Hills Correctional Facility (Fine et al., 2021), and then fan out widely in dissemination and organizing across the country. Projects can be rooted in a broad-based fight for the city, as in the research of homeless activists in Hungary who formed a collective with Eva Udvarhelyi and Marianne Dosa (2019) through "The City Is for All" and that of immigrant and undocumented bicycle food delivery workers in New York City who are fighting, at once, for immigration, labor, racial, and transportation justice in their CPAR collaboration with Do Lee (2018).

CPAR projects are also developed transnationally to bear witness to injustice across borders and the rising resistance movements that dot the globe. For instance, transnational researchers, activists, and artists working with Caro Munoz-Proto (2009) have curated an online archive of photographs, letters, and *testimonios* of lives against violence called Memoscopio (https://www.publicscienceproject.org/memoscopio). After gathering videos across the globe, while accompanying the World March for Peace and Nonviolence (https://en.theworldmarch.org/), the collective gathered thousands of photos, selfies, and pictures of the largest paella ever produced in Spain and interviews with mothers, fathers, children, grandparents, former soldiers, activists, students, peasants, and artists, all of whom contributed images and testimonies and then assembled them into Memoscopio as a transnational "evidence" archive of nonviolence freedom dreams.

In each of these spaces—all anchored by people who have been denied housing or banished to the pathologized margins and people who have been locked up or spoken for, exploited, and written out of the moral contract—there is a bold commitment to "no research about us without us"; a sharp critique of "normalcy," those at the "center," and dominant lies; a fierce dedication to inquiry by, for, and about those who have been targeted by oppressive policies; and a sweet range of demands for a different future, built from the ground up.

- How might engaging the arts open new lines of collaborative inquiry and aesthetic provocation? CPAR projects that braid research into social movements and the arts demonstrate new ways of seeing. While there is a long tradition of using the arts to amplify findings, many research collectives have engaged the arts as analysis, as a way of revealing patterns within the data that might be otherwise obscured. Madeline Fox (2015) and the research collectives she has worked with have developed analysis techniques using embodiment and Playback Theater to surface and theorize emotions and affect provoked by their data. Deepening avenues for participation within the research collective, these techniques have been extended into and also expand participation in dissemination stages, wherein Fox and her youth colleagues pause performances of their findings for audience interpretation and theorizing. Other examples include Caitlin Cahill and her colleagues David Quijada Cerecer and Matt Bradley (2010), who collaborated with the Mestizo Arts & Activism Collective to launch the "Dreaming No Judgment" project, weaving participatory research, poetry, mural art, and spoken word by and for immigrant youth and artists in Salt Lake City. Leconté Dill (2015) and her analysis collective have adapted a version of poetic inquiry, creating "research poems" to interpret their interview narratives. Wendy Luttrell (2020) has gathered a decade's worth of photographs taken by working-class children (from sixth grade forward), creating a process through which youth documented and interpreted care worlds in their childhoods through late adolescence. In these projects, CPAR is braided into the arts, enabling the voices, outrage, talents, and visions of children and youth to be heard unmediated.

- Where does CPAR live? CPAR is by no means the province of the academy. Some projects are located primarily in the university, but many are begun and remain in the communities outside the academy. Brooklyn-based Girls for Gender Equity (Smith et al., 2011) launched a powerful creative inquiry project by young women documenting rampant sexual harassment in their schools and streets. Using ethnographic methods and results from their survey of more than 1,000 youth, they eventually produced a "guidebook" from their findings called *Hey, Shorty: A Guide to Combating Sexual Harassment and Violence in Schools and on the Streets.* Black and Pink, an activist organization of and for formerly and presently incarcerated people who identify as LGBTQIA+, initiated a survey of and by LGBTQIA+ people in prison by soliciting questions for the survey from members behind bars through their monthly newspaper. Using the questions to draft the survey, they then incorporated the survey into a later edition of the newspaper. Their report "Coming Out of Concrete Closets: A Report on Black & Pink's National LGBTQ Prisoner Survey" (Lydon et al., 2015) was distributed to their incarcerated membership and used by queer activists and prison abolitionists.

CPAR projects have been launched in schools, neighborhoods, community-based organizations, prisons, social service agencies, detention centers, and beyond. Each of these contexts brings opportunities and limits. What is important is that the university should never be considered the "obvious" site of the research because it can be alienating to members of communities that have been historically excluded. At the same time, universities have massive resources in terms of space, technology, libraries, prestige, and opportunities that should be opened and leveraged for just research (Rubin, Ayala, & Zaal, 2017).

PARTICIPATORY RESEARCH AS A TOOL OF STRUGGLE AND SOLIDARITY IN CONTENTIOUS TIMES

It should be clear at this point that CPAR projects have been birthed from various social movements, community-based organizations, and critical academic traditions; feminist groups (Brydon-Miller & Greenwood, 2006; Maguire, 1987) and immigrant rights organizations; queer movements and organizations run by and for formerly incarcerated people; and the Movement for Black Lives and #MeToo. CPAR has a long history in disability justice movements and with practitioners of critical pedagogy and critical legal studies. Labor movements are increasingly gathering data from, with, and by workers using CPAR, as are those struggling for dignity and housing for those who identify as housing insecure or homeless (Billies, 2017; Udvarhelyi & Dosa, 2019).

The projects we have highlighted represent unique and provocative works framed by a range of critical perspectives, and we invite you to follow the leads they provide so you might appreciate the wide variations—and deep common commitments—that span the field. We make no attempt to be comprehensive. These projects have been born and are perched at a critical angle, addressing questions of power, inequity, and radical possibilities, producing works that are intellectually and aesthetically provocative.

CHALLENGES AND JOYS

Every CPAR project is a freedom dream, a project that hopes that evidence will matter to policy makers and people with power and that illuminating it will bring justice to communities in struggle. While it is rare that one project ever quite reaches this horizon, the collective journey brings with it an incredible power, with ripples that can turn into waves. Indeed, CPAR limits are easy to name but hard to categorize. Projects often begin with ambitious goals of dismantling an enraging injustice, transforming a law or policy, shifting school culture, stopping state violence, freeing children in detention centers, and ending domestic violence, knowing, of course, that the research will almost always fall short. We have far too much "evidence" at this point: Injustice is not simply a cognitive problem. That said, CPAR projects dream big and contribute significantly. But it never feels like enough.

Challenges are numerous (Guishard, 2009). CPAR projects by nature are rooted in the perspectives of those most impacted, and they are organized around change. The systems and institutions upholding unjust policies are rarely invested in "feedback" and too often try to silence the insights, dynamics, and tensions lifted by the research. It is easy to anticipate that the findings of a CPAR project may be ignored by a single institution, and so we have learned to build expansive solidarity networks for our research collectives, nesting a school-based project, for example, within a lattice of community-based organizations and activist groups that can push back and support the research in these contexts.

Challenges within CPAR can also be internal to the research collective; intragroup dynamics emerge that unchecked can undermine the trust of the collective. Someone may tire of "studying" rather than demanding justice. Outside life can interrupt members' abilities to participate. Sometimes, internal pressures impact the collective, and coresearchers may fear retaliation by school officials, the police, or other authorities whose practices are being challenged by the research. Some grow weary of government or elites who will never listen. Leaders of schools or police departments, mayors, or wardens of prisons often do not care what "the people" want. They may concede with incremental change, but institutions fight hard to sustain themselves, and those with power fight hardest. Participation—or "listening tours"—have become a neoliberal fad, without any commitment to sharing power, reciprocity, or radical transformation.

In universities, institutional review boards (IRBs) or ethics boards often do not respect the participation of community members; funders often do not want to pay for child care, transportation, or labor of everyday people; journals do not like to publish long lists of contributors; university faculty may not want to supervise dissertations where collaborators not affiliated with a university are recognized as "authors"; or hiring and tenure and promotion committees may get stuck on artificial binaries, only recognizing the activism and not the scholarship. Or on the contrary, academics build careers while coresearchers continue living in conditions that are unchanged. These are not dirty little secrets in the trade; these are the dynamics we all must confront.

Regardless of scale, CPAR commitments call on us to dive into the heart of the challenges and worries we face in our work, what Lac in Lac and Fine (2018) called "the good, the bad, and the ugly" in her autoethnographic account of doing PAR as a graduate student, as a way to continually undo colonizing and supremacist practices in our research, critiques of the consequences of the massive appropriation of participation by corporations, multinational firms, and global institutions, such as the World Bank and the International Monetary Fund, interested in superficial and tokenistic gestures of participation, devoid of analyses of power, and not at all committed to deep and transformational participation (Cooke & Kothari, 2001; Su, 2017).

And yet, time and again, in the past and now, in prisons in New York and mining towns in Appalachia, in communities in El Salvador and Hungary, in New Orleans and Salt Lake City, collectives of CPAR scholars and activists have managed to smuggle critically engaged projects into cracks of opportunities, occupying a space for inquiry, gathering people who know—in their bellies—how injustice thrives, and they have produced significant work that reveals important critical wisdom about what is and what could be (Billies, 2017; Fine, 2017; Halkovic & Greene, 2015; Stoudt et al., 2011).

We close this section, however, with a soft warning: No one—graduate students or faculty—should simply decide "I am going to do a CPAR project in this community" without knowing the people, the needs, the history of research, and the ongoing struggles the community has faced. Further, you should always be aware of how the university might be "using" these projects to brand how multiracial and community oriented they are, even when the IRB tries to stop the work or youth researchers are hassled by the university police. It is all predictable and our responsibility when launching a CPAR project in unwelcoming terrain.

The truth is, especially now as COVID-19 has illuminated with such extreme clarity the degree to which White supremacy continues to structure and maintain the ongoing systems of oppression that shape the deep inequalities of our society, it can feel like a luxury, or even irresponsible, to be studying injustice when the causes, consequences, and alternatives seem so obvious and the need for mass mobilization and action so urgent. This moment calls on us now more than ever to design research as part of transformative change. CPAR offers a praxis of research that allows us to stand together in solidarity, bear witness in the community, engage freedom struggles, and produce, with humility, research that dares to tell a different story, one that imagines another more just tomorrow.

6 METHODOLOGICAL INTEGRITY

Let's begin our conversation of methodological integrity for critical participatory action research (CPAR) with the framework articulated by Levitt et al. (2017) in *American Psychologist*. For Levitt et al., integrity encapsulates the trustworthiness of the interpretations forwarded by researchers, as well as the design's fidelity to the subject matter and utility in achieving research goals. They argued that

> fidelity to the subject matter is the process by which researchers select procedures that develop and maintain allegiance to the phenomenon under study . . . [and] is improved when researchers collect data from sources that can shed light upon variations in the phenomenon . . . when [researchers] recognize and are transparent about the influence of their own perspectives . . . on data collection . . . and their analytic process. (p. 32)

Let's begin there.

https://doi.org/10.1037/0000241-006
Essentials of Critical Participatory Action Research, by M. Fine and M. E. Torre

FIDELITY AND DIVERSITY

How are these commitments embodied and enacted in CPAR? Let us consider the three ways fidelity and diversity are woven into CPAR projects: theoretically, in terms of design, and in the analysis and dissemination phases. First, CPAR projects grow from and through a diverse set of standpoints and curiosities, theoretical perspectives, and lived experiences held by the various members of the research collective. Second, we seek diversity in evidence. Statistics, maps, archival and historical material, autoethnography, visual material, ethnographic reflections, and narratives are typically and intentionally gathered from a wide range of sources and a broad range of positionalities to shed light on variations within. Third, our participatory analyses marinate in dialogues about power and difference, divergent interpretations, and a search for new understandings. Seeking not consensus but democratic knowledge production, researchers with widely varying biographies share their interpretations hatched at the intersection of statistical associations and rich generative narratives. They work through the complex assemblage of evidence in deliberative dialogues, across contested perspectives, sparked by deep curiosities, thrills, and aches borne in their biographies, confronting statistical surprises, immersing themselves in dialogues and disagreements, being motivated by patterns and contradictions, and being obligated to serious, attentive listening.

TO BE OF USE: ACTION, TRANSFORMATION, AND PROVOCATION

Levitt et al. (2017) recommended a second element of methodological integrity that involves "utility in achieving research goals" through the contextualization of data, evidence as a "catalyst for insight," and offering "meaningful contributions" with "coherence among the findings" (p. 34). On this strand of integrity, it seems CPAR is ambitious in its aims even though we may fall a bit short of hoped-for goals. That is, our evidence is rich and often quite useful in its contributions, but findings sometimes point to contradictions, complicating tidy notions of "coherence." As with the What's Your Issue? study (Torre et al., 2018), where the data gathered fundamentally transformed conventional thinking about gender and sexuality dynamics and their intersections with race, the findings are meaningful and provocative to scholars, educators, activists, policy makers, and LGBTQIA+ young people and their families; still, there is a vibrant (in)coherence to the findings because, indeed, the variation within the community is wild and enormous. In the Changing Minds study (Fine et al., 2021), we documented that college in prison massively reduces recidivism, supports women's growth and development, enhances their children's likelihoods of going on to college, softens the disciplinary culture in the prison, and saves taxpayer dollars. The evaluation determined that the college program was a tremendous success. Yet, almost 25 years later, the noncompetitive Pell Grant dollars that supported college programs are still denied to people in prison. Much has changed in the movement for college in prison—philanthropic support, private sector initiatives, university partnerships, and vibrant organizing efforts led by formerly incarcerated people—but the fundamental policy change has not been realized. Our Changing Minds report is available online and is downloaded frequently by state commissioners of corrections looking for evidence-based strategies to reduce recidivism, but the exclusionary laws remain.

One must be humble about the reach of research in contentious times and remember that research is but one element in the struggle for justice. In today's deeply inequitable world, community-based participatory research is most powerful when linked to organizing movements, local popular education, litigation, and policy change (Massey & Barreras, 2013).

CPAR TOUCHSTONES FOR INTEGRITY AND ACCOUNTABILITY

As a supplement to fidelity and utility, CPAR offers a few additional epistemological touchstones for methodological integrity and accountability:

- First, CPAR projects are essentially fueled by what Sandra Harding (1991) called "strong objectivity," challenging the belief that academics are the only "experts" and facilitating instead the deliberate pooling of diverse standpoints to design inquiry. The broad range of researchers amplifies an expansive and layered understanding of the issue under study and accountability to various forms of expertise.

- Second, in the early knowledge-sharing phase of CPAR projects, co-researchers within the participatory contact zone share insights and experiences, biography, and autoethnography, speaking through reflexivity and vulnerability about their relationships to the issue under study. In so doing, they fundamentally reshape how to think about the issue and recalibrate the angle of inquiry, clearing a dialogic and reflexive space where no one standpoint can overdetermine the direction of the inquiry.

- Third, CPAR takes seriously the wisdom generated in pilots, or "bad drafts," of research designs, methods, or protocols when the process of research is intentionally slowed down and democratically scrutinized by those most experienced with the issue under study. This dialogic process humbles academic frameworks and enacts strategies to decolonize methods and ways of knowing.

- Fourth, participatory analysis typical in CPAR takes nothing for granted; no constructs are assumed to be self-evident. Research activities are designed so all members of the collective can collaboratively pull apart, dissect, and reassemble constructs, variables, and dynamics, to enhance our construct validity. Rethinking common psychological constructs by the very people psychologists typically write about rather than with is both theoretically and ethically generative.

- Fifth, CPAR offers spaces for community conversations and dialogues about evidence—statistical, thematic, or within a single life—moments that expand expertise beyond the research team, looping more and more participants with relevant experiences into the evolving questions produced by the scientific process.

- Sixth, the layered richness of most CPAR data creates openings for what I (MF; Fine, 2017) have called "provocative generalizability" when we present our findings to communities and audiences in universities and organizations across the country. We hope to spark not a technical sense of statistical generalizability but a resonant wide-awakeness (Greene, 1977) and action across time and space—whether about policing or the presence of "out" teachers in schools, the impact of college in prison, or the state separation of families.

- Seventh, CPAR urges a scholarly "response-ability" to hear, include, and represent participants' phenomenological desires. Much psychological research has historically been an imperial act, a colonizing project, in which those of us in the academy laid "our" theories over, at times smothering, "others'" lives (Teo, 2010).

CPAR offers a humble path for decolonizing research, one that stitches an ethics of reciprocity and accountability into research designs and creates opportunities to democratize knowledge and provoke evidence-driven wide-awakeness and re-cognition.

EVALUATING CPAR: HOW DO YOU KNOW WHETHER IT IS GOOD ENOUGH?

We are often asked how we know whether CPAR is valid. If coresearchers are so familiar with the issue under study, might they bring their biases into the work? Or, more skeptically (and dismissively), is this just advocacy or journalism? Let us first dispense with the bias charge. CPAR recognizes that all people are situated, with lines of vision influenced by situated knowledge. Our biographies, our communities of origin, and our current positions place us in different kinds of communities, relationships, and conversations, with access to some experiences and in full ignorance of others. CPAR is an ambitious science project in which varying perspectives sit beside and work through their orientations, listen attentively to alternative frameworks, and generate questions that boil over at the messy intersections.

To the question "Is it good enough?" we offer thoughts on how we evaluate our work and that of others. To begin, we must admit that in the current neoliberal moment, calls for participation have become a buzzword. You should be suspect. We are surrounded by many weak or, worse, unethical inquiries that claim to be participatory. Some projects use children's voices in ways that are self-serving or, worse, exploitive, as in forms of "poverty porn" or "immigration porn," wherein children are represented as victims, not agents, resisters, or people with their own minds, desires, and voices. Multinational corporations deploy marketing strategies they consider "participatory" as they lace people's words into already formed corporate agendas "as if" they came from the desires of "the people." This is not participatory practice; it is appropriation and tokenism. Projects that invite youth in but insist that they speak in scripts are already overwritten by adults and are not participatory. Projects that promise to "include silenced voices" or "give voice" but fail to address the structural conditions that marginalize or silence are unacceptable and, even if "well intentioned," simply reproduce the epistemological violence against which CPAR organized.

That said, we strive for "good-enough" CPAR, drawing on Winnicott's (1973) notion of "good-enough mothering." We look to see to what extent the research enacts designs informed by critical theory, cultivates and is led by deep and inclusive participation, builds a research culture that facilitates strong objectivity, engages in collective reflexivity, works through diversity in analysis, and aims to "be of use" in larger projects of transformation. When assessing other PAR or CPAR projects, we bring humility to a set of inquiries:

- At the level of *C* for critical, to what extent does critical theory—explicit attention to and analysis of power—frame the work? Are lives represented as intersectional and complex? Are they situated in a decolonizing history and recognition of how social structures and policies have contributed to oppression and privilege? Or are people represented as "free" and "autonomous," dangling, neoliberal autonomous subjects untethered to policy, social arrangements, or the current historical moment? Does the writing challenge dominant lies and offer up other ways to review social arrangements? From whose perspective is the social science story being told?

- At the level of *P* for participatory, to what extent is there deep, wide, and fully inclusive participation and direction by those most impacted by the topic under study. Who is on the research team, who is not, who is excluded—and why? If research team members have left, how has the project attended to the reasons for leaving? There are times when life gets in the way of full involvement in a CPAR project, cutting short or interrupting full participation. On the Morris Justice Project (Stoudt et al., 2016), some of the young men had to step back at the point of data collection for fear that the police would retaliate against them for distributing surveys. On the What's Your Issue? project, there were moments when housing or health struggles interfered with full participation by some of our research team members. Sometimes, people just need time off from studying the injustices they live daily. There is a liberatory aspect of studying intimate injustice—and a vulnerability aspect. CPAR projects need to anticipate and honor these temporary—or longer—departures, support coresearchers, enable moments for self-care and collective care, and welcome people back when they are ready to return.

- At the level of *A* for action, we are interested in how the researchers plan to move the findings into action, policy, organizing, theatre, popular education, scholarship, and teaching. To whom are the researchers accountable? We are interested in how the researchers intend the work to intervene in the world as it is and as it could be.

- And at the level of *R* for research, we ask, in the spirit of Levitt et al. (2017), have various forms of evidence been brought into the conversation? To what extent do the communities involved trust and potentially rely on the material that has been gathered? Are there attempts to find counterstories and points of dissension in the material? Are groups presented as heterogeneous and intersectional, affected by social structures but also agentic and resilient? Do the analytic codes represent well enough the intentions of the respondents? Do the authors reproduce categories, victim-blaming attributions, and/or stereotypes about the community, or do they work to challenge these classic psychological stories? Did the reader learn something new from reading or engaging with the research products? Do some conclusions or insights resonate across different communities and contexts, provoking reflection and/or action? Is there evidence that the material was gathered in ways that were ethical and attentive to the vulnerabilities of the community?

Methodological integrity in CPAR is a complex project because the tight and well-maintained borders set up around conventional research methods are porous and fluid in CPAR. CPAR projects are relational, nested in movements and social theory, situated across university and community, and designed for scholarly validity and community-based utility. To assess integrity, we must peek under the covers to see how the research attaches to theory and movements, how deep the participation is, how systematic is the analysis, how response-able are the final products, and how accountable it is to the hunger, vulnerabilities, and power of the communities under siege.

7 WRITING PROCESS AND RESEARCH PRODUCTS

We turn now to the writing up of critical participatory action research (CPAR), thinking through how the material is presented in varied venues: in book chapters and journals, of course, but also and more urgently in community meetings, in courtrooms, on websites, and in performance, policy, and public spaces. A chapter on writing CPAR touches on questions big and small. To begin with, there are questions of audience. To whom is the collective writing— judges, policy makers, community activists, educators, youth, lawyers, scholars, other researchers? CPAR has a wide range of communities with whom, and to whom, we write—and each project holds an obligation to revisit its purpose and draft materials to be "of use" to those audiences that matter. This means thinking about accessibility, language, jargon, and questions of power. What will authorship look like? Will you alphabetize? Will you feature the most distinguished academic first? Will you author the piece as the CPAR Collective? Will you write in Spanish or in braille? Will you include cartoons or films? Will you present the piece as street theatre or an amicus brief for the courts?

https://doi.org/10.1037/0000241-007
Essentials of Critical Participatory Action Research, by M. Fine and M. E. Torre

These initial questions quickly move into further questions about form: How might the findings be presented in ways that make sense to different audiences? Will you fold your findings into policy documents, scholarly articles, or organizing brochures? Will you emblazon them on T-shirts or buttons? Will you use them to create spoken word pieces, videos, archives, bumper stickers, postcards, or websites? CPAR projects are nested at the intersection of so many audiences; figuring out "how to be of use" is an ongoing discussion that typically inspires not just one research "product" but many. Do you want to raise consciousness or change a law? Do you want to challenge a stereotype or affirm the rich wisdom of the community? Do you want to educate children or remind elites of their responsibilities? What kinds of products should be created is entirely up to the research collective and is generally decided by the various agendas of the research and coresearchers involved. Some projects release findings to lawyers, as the Morris Justice Project did in efforts to inform the legal team and community organizing against the use of stop and frisk (Stoudt et al., 2016), or publish an official policy white paper with multiple coauthors, as we did in the Changing Minds study, sending our report on college in prison to the governor of every state in the country and every state legislator in New York State (Fine et al., 2001). Also wanting to create a campaign of support, we printed and sent out more than 1,000 postcards, each featuring a quote from women in the prison college program, children of women in the college program, or corrections officers, each with statistics that demonstrated that participation in college reduced recidivism.

Some research teams host community events to unveil their findings or perform the findings, as we did in the Echoes of Brown project, where youth and adults created and performed their interpretations of the large-scale quantitative survey through spoken word and dance (Fine et al., 2004). Our hope was to reveal the unfulfilled promise of *Brown v. Board of Education* (1954) and provoke audiences to take action against the inadequate implementation of integration 50 years after 1954. Most projects also publish academic papers, alongside more creative research products that are relevant to audiences and communities that are prioritized by the research collective.

As research products are created, the questions of authorship must be revisited. Who writes, who edits, who presents? Ideally, the answer is all of us. At the Public Science Project, we have evolved an ethical commitment that everyone who serves on the research team is an author on our first set of reports, papers, and products, recognizing that there are multiple ways to contribute, all of which should be credited. Sometimes, collective writing starts with a "bad draft" created by a member or a subset of the team that is then circulated and reconstructed. At other times, groups outline ideas and then interview each other using prompts from the outline and then stitch the interviews to craft drafts of the writing (Stoudt et al., 2016). Truth be told, not everyone loves writing. "You write, and we'll critique it" is the oft-spoken response to "How should we write together?" It has been our practice to strive to keep opening opportunities for writing by demystifying the process and creating accessible ways to engage, often beginning with talking. No matter how first drafts emerge, everyone reads (or listens to), reviews, critiques, and helps with rewrites. Each person gives what they can to the work. And when we present at scholarly, organizing, or community sessions, as many as can, as best as we can, show up.

Often, after the first round of products is produced, CPAR collectives decide that members of the group can go on to create their own documents and products under their own authorship as long as they inform the collective and cite the collective research. Conversations about authorship and public recognition should be ongoing throughout the life of a project because members may make different decisions depending on social and political contexts and statuses. Collective members may want to use their real names; others may choose to use pseudonyms or go unnamed. We have experienced colleagues who decide to use their names at the beginning of a project, sometimes even their photos and/or voices in mixed-media products, and then as political contexts shift or their situation changes, they have changed their minds. It is important to build in times for "check-ins" and think through alternative means of recognition and credit. In addition to shared authorship, we believe that everyone should be paid—we are all contributing labor. Those of us in the academy may forgo payment when the research is part of our salaried work, but coresearchers should be compensated financially so that the work of the research does not take away from needed paid hours elsewhere. Some projects compensate with gift cards, college credits, or other resources that specific contexts might have. However it happens, creative attention must be paid to make sure everyone is able to receive compensation, including those without social security numbers and those in vulnerable situations.

People have asked where the narratives, data, and videos live when the project is over. Again, this is a conversation for the collective to have early and throughout the research process. When the research collective is not tied to an institution, they can hold the empirical materials and decide what is sacred and what should and should not be made public. When members are connected to institutions, the collective then has to decide how and where things are stored and how to navigate access and for whom. A participatory project conducted by formerly incarcerated college students, focused on the barriers they encounter and the gifts they bring to the university, remains online at the Prisoner Reentry Institute, a reentry program at John Jay College of Criminal Justice (see "Higher Education and Reentry: The Gifts They Bring," by Tejawi et al., 2013). The oral histories collected by a collective of undocumented and Deferred Action for Childhood Arrivals activists who fought for the New Jersey Dream Act are being held by The Center for Undocumented Students at Saint Peter's University (Ayala et al., 2020). Increasingly, however, with state surveillance evermore focused on punishing and criminalizing marginalized communities, scholars and activists have decided not to take notes or to destroy the tapes so that no voice recognition technology can be applied and no tapes can be subpoenaed. Discussions about vulnerabilities, erasure, and the importance of preserving evidence about the legacies of struggle lie at the heart of CPAR.

Finally, as we write, we must contend with questions about how we authentically represent points of rupture or disagreements among us. The easy answer is it depends—on the intention of the work, the target audience, and the dynamics of the research team. In official policy documents, we tend not to discuss tensions or disagreements among the research team, although there can be a dissenting report. In academic or even community products, we may reference "rich discussions and disagreement about this interpretation" or the "many interpretations for this set of findings." In essays that are specifically about critical participatory epistemologies, methodologies, and research practice—like this book—we spend time unpacking those moments because, in fact, they are generative and creative. They are also instructive for researchers new to critical participatory work. Because dissent is an important part of CPAR and understood to open fertile spaces for analysis and interpretation, there should be mechanisms for representing these fracture points as moments of knowledge production in methods, results, conclusions, or even, if need be, a footnote.

Regardless of whether we are producing creative or traditional research products, we seek to present the research in a mode that honors and resonates with our collaborating community. In 2001, when we published the policy report of Changing Minds (Fine et al., 2021), we brought the graphic designer's draft layout into the prison, and our colleagues inside were clear that they did not want a report with prison bars, austere depressing images, or bold black letters; they wanted something beautiful, filled with life and relationships, critique and community: "It should have lipstick!" And so, the pages were interspersed with photo strips, letters written in longhand, and postcards that could be sent in the mail.

When we published an academic chapter on challenging stereotypes called "Refusing to Check the Box" (Fine et al., 2018), drawn from What's Your Issue? and focused on young people's rejection of labels and simplistic binaries, the article opened with a photo of our coresearcher Alex—actually a close up of Alex's quite pregnant belly that he sent the collective when he was not allowed to fly for our last gathering. The chapter then followed with narratives and statistics, telling a story of youth critique and self-determination, ending with banners from the survey in which respondents re-presented themselves in their own words. Questions, conversations, and collective decision making about writing and representation are particularly important when academics (in our case, psychologists) are trusted enough to research and write alongside people in struggle, theorizing systems from which we unequally benefit and suffer.

Participatory writing is a process of collective discovery, laced with trust, revision, and respect. It is a journey peppered with questions of authorship, contributions, responsibility, consequences, recognition, language, vulnerability, representation, and (mis)representation. And there are important conversations about purpose, products, and writing styles for the collective to consider when you begin:

- Will the writing be academic prose with citations?
- Will you include slang? Spanish? The language of the participants?
- Will it integrate poetry, art, and local artifacts?
- How will you create a process for review and feedback if not everyone is involved in each draft?
- Will you write in multiple "voices," or will you try to create "one voice" from multiple perspectives?
- Might there be a dissenting epilogue?
- If it is a report, will you seek critical and loving endorsements from a range of stakeholders?

From a project's start, it is important to have an open conversation and acknowledge the different ways people contribute; it is not just "writing" that qualifies someone as an author. Writing, experience, analysis, and practice all matter. It is important that the project builds in creative methods that scaffold everyone's participation and growth, allowing coresearchers to encourage each other to push past what is comfortable or feels "natural" to them, whether that is reading statistical output, writing, or public speaking. What is important here is that credit for contribution does not hang on any one way of participating—for instance, writing.

One of our publication traditions at the Public Science Project requires that everyone on the research team is listed as an author (in whatever way they feel comfortable) on a first collectively produced research product or, sometimes, a set of projects. You will notice some long author lists in the References. After the team feels like the products that the collective has together decided to produce are complete, individuals or smaller subsets of coresearchers are typically free to publish articles, chapters, white papers, brochures, fliers, or zines on their own—with two friendly requests: that they cite the original full group document, and when possible, they should discuss with members of the group the subsequent products and, if desired, present drafts to the original larger group for feedback—and blessings. This process in practice is ethical, thoughtful, careful, and respectful—as research and writing should be.

EPILOGUE

Critical PAR in Crisis: An Epistemic Offering Toward Solidarity

In the early days of the COVID-19 crisis, writer Arundhati Roy asked,

> What is this thing that has happened to us? It's a virus, yes. In and of itself it holds no moral brief. But it is definitely more than a virus. . . . And in the midst of this terrible despair, it offers us a chance to rethink the doomsday machine we have built for ourselves. Nothing could be worse than a return to normality. Historically, pandemics have forced humans to break with the past and imagine their world anew. This one is no different. It is a portal, a gateway between one world and the next. (Roy, 2020, para. 46–48)

In the mo(u)rning after COVID-19, in a nation of ongoing police murders of Black people, a nation that separates immigrant children from families and holds them in cages, a nation that refuses science and denies climate change, social researchers will hopefully realize we cannot go back to "normality," as Arundhati Roy warned. We cannot continue to presume we "know" and that others do not. We cannot continue the fantasy that academics have answers and enjoy a monopoly on knowledge and objectivity, that anyone can live a life separate from others' suffering. Through the portal of massive death, illness, and economic despair, all starkly and grotesquely stratified by race and class, the gulf of inequities that pave our nation and make it easy for some of

https://doi.org/10.1037/0000241-008
Essentials of Critical Participatory Action Research, by M. Fine and M. E. Torre

us and impossible for others widens evermore. We can no longer deny that some communities and people live with "preexisting conditions," raced and classed inequities baked into our national history and current policies, and are thereby more vulnerable to the virus; more targeted by racial injustice, privatization, testing, state violence, and deportation; and more exposed to the impacts of trauma. Our privilege and epistemologies of ignorance have been exposed. We can never again say we did not know its depths.

Many have turned to us at the Public Science Project during this crisis seeking a praxis of critical participatory action research (CPAR) with which to build solidarities with communities under siege. They desire rapid response techniques and also long-term methods as ways to fight for justice through inquiry with people in prison, mixed-status immigrant families, LGBTQIA+ young people struggling with challenging families, women quarantined in homes with domestic violence, educators trying to decolonize and build culturally responsive curricula, families living in fear of state violence, teens studying inequities in access to online education, rural advocates documenting sweet instances of mutual aid in times of crisis, Black Americans in the South advocating for participatory inquiries with local courts, and hospitals and schools now exposed for gross and ongoing racial inequities. We must recognize that across lines of race, class, neighborhood, religion, sexuality, (dis)ability, and immigration status, we are deeply interdependent. No one is "safer" when those most vulnerable fall; we are simply next. Walls do nothing but deny relationships that already exist. White people must stop calling the police on people of color; elites must not be allowed to continue accumulating wealth and power as so many die in plain sight. And perhaps as fundamentally, this crisis has illuminated our throbbing desires to connect and the planet's ability to "heal" when humanity's abuses stop. If ignored, these simple facts will kill us. Alternatively, we could honor the tremendous loss and recognize the ways our social relations are a gift.

Inequities render us all vulnerable in the long run, and if we commit instead to solidarities, mutual aid, and cooperation, we could set a course for a different future. For those of us in the academy and in psychology, it is time to build research collectives for solidarity and research justice, informed by our common and distinct knowledge, designed to strengthen our collective well-being, rooted in the wisdom of those most impacted, with unwanted expertise about living in conditions of inequity.

After 25 years of experience with PAR, we are confident that research can be organized through solidarities to build collective imagination, strength, and healing and to build collective immunity, with progressive ethics of equity, participation, inclusion, and democratic praxis. With this volume, we introduced a methodologically expansive legacy overlooked in our history, and we invite a restorative reflection on the harm psychology has caused and the repair work that CPAR can accompany.

Looking forward to a post–COVID-19 world, we know, of course, that research is just one small piece of social transformation—but it can be meaningful. We build collective immunity and power by growing ligaments that connect universities, community organizations, and movements for social justice. We build collective immunity by reaching back with elders and forward with youth and Indigenous, immigrant, coal-mining, and queer communities, communities who have long known struggle, ones we are a part of and ones that we are not. Together we can learn how to move through the pain, isolation, and despair. We can learn how to build power by challenging the very marrow of oppressive systems and institutions and unjust privilege. We can build modest and daring paths of liberation for ourselves and each other. We can, in the words of Gerald Vizenor (1999), create a collective praxis of "survivance" among us. Together, we can, with humility and perseverance, build research and campaigns for a more just tomorrow. We wish you well as you venture into CPAR and begin carving new participatory pathways of socially just research.

References

American Psychological Association. (2020). *Publication manual of the American Psychological Association* (7th ed.). https://doi.org/10.1037/0000165-000

Anzaldúa, G. (1987). *Borderlands/La Frontera: The new mestiza.* Aunt Lute Books.

Anzaldúa, G. E. (2002). (Un)natural bridges, (un)safe spaces. In G. E. Anzaldúa & A. Keating (Eds.), *This bridge we call home: Radical visions for transformation* (pp. 1–5). Routledge.

Appadurai, A. (2006). The right to research. *Globalisation, Societies and Education, 4*(2), 167–177. https://doi.org/10.1080/14767720600750696

Ayala, J., Cammarota, J., Berta-Avila, M. I., Rivera, M., Rodriguez, L. F., & Torre, M. E. (2018). *PAR EntreMundos: A pedagogy for the Americas.* Peter Lang.

Ayala, J., Fine, M., Mendez, M. del C., Mendoza, A. N. J., Rivera, J. C. G., Finesurrey, S., Villeda, A., Thelusca, H., Mena, V., Azzam, K., Galletta, A., Houston, A., jones, v., & Mungo, D. (2020). ENCUENTROS: Decolonizing the academy and mobilizing for justice. *Qualitative Inquiry.* Advance online publication. https://doi.org/10.1177/1077800420960161

Azzam, K., Galletta, A., Houston, A., jones, v., & Mungo, D. (2020). Tracing history for the pulse of liberation. In J. Ayala, M. Fine, M. del C. Mendez, A. N. J. Mendoza, J. C. G. Rivera, S. Finesurrey, A. Villeda, H. Thelusca, V. Mena, K. Azzam, A. Galletta, A. Houston, v. jones, & D. Mungo (Eds.), ENCUENTROS: Decolonizing the academy and mobilizing for justice. *Qualitative Inquiry.* Advance online publication. https://doi.org/10.1177/1077800420960161

Billies, M. (2017). How can psychology support low-income LGBTGNC liberation? In S. Grabe (Ed.), *Women's human rights: A social psychological perspective on resistance, liberation and justice* (pp. 40–69). Oxford University Press.

Brown v. Board of Education, 347 U.S. 483 (1954). https://www.oyez.org/cases/1940-1955/347us483

Brydon-Miller, M., & Greenwood, D. (2006). A re-examination of the relationship between action research and human subjects review process. *Action Research, 4*(1), 117–128. https://doi.org/10.1177/1476750306060582

Cahill, C. (2010). 'Why do they hate us?' Reframing immigration through participatory action research. *Area*, *42*(2), 152–161. https://doi.org/10.1111/j.1475-4762.2009.00929.x

Cahill, C., Quijada Cerecer, D., & Bradley, M. (2010). "Dreaming of . . .": Reflections on participatory action research as a feminist praxis of critical hope. *Affilia*, *25*(4), 406–416. https://doi.org/10.1177/0886109910384576

Cahill, C., Sultana, F., & Pain, R. (2015). Participatory ethics: Politics, practices, and institutions. *ACME: An International e-Journal for Critical Geographies*, *6*(3), 304–318.

Cammarota, J., & Fine, M. (2008). *Revolutionizing education: Youth participatory action research in motion*. Routledge.

Caraballo, L., Lozenski, B. D., Lyiscott, J. J., & Morrell, E. (2017). YPAR and critical epistemologies: Rethinking education research. *Review of Research in Education*, *41*(1), 311–336. https://doi.org/10.3102/0091732X16686948

Carolissen, R., Canham, H., Fourie, E., Graham, T., Segalo, P., & Bowen, B. (2017). Epistemic resistance toward diversity: Teaching community psychology as a decolonial project. *South African Journal of Community Psychology*, *47*(4), 495–505. https://doi.org/10.1177/0081246317739203

Collins, P. H. (1991). *Black feminist thought: Knowledge, consciousness, and the politics of empowerment*. Routledge.

Collins, P. H. (2012). Social inequality, power, and politics: Intersectionality and American pragmatism in dialogue. *The Journal of Speculative Philosophy*, *26*(2), 442–457. https://doi.org/10.5325/jspecphil.26.2.0442

Combahee River Collective. (1977). *The Combahee River Collective statement*. https://combaheerivercollective.weebly.com/the-combahee-river-collective-statement.html

Cooke, B., & Kothari, U. (2001). *Participation: The new tyranny?* Zed.

Crenshaw, K. (1989). Demarginalizing the intersection of race and sex: A Black feminist critique of antidiscrimination doctrine. *University of Chicago Legal Forum*, *1989*(1), 8. https://chicagounbound.uchicago.edu/cgi/viewcontent.cgi?article=1052&context=uclf

Crenshaw, K. (2008). Mapping the margins: Intersectionality, identity politics and violence against Women of Color. In A. Bailey & C. Cuomo (Eds.), *The feminist philosophy reader* (pp. 279–309). McGraw-Hill.

de Sousa Santos, B. (2014). *Epistemologies of the South: Justice against epistemicide*. Routledge.

Dill, L. J. (2015). Poetic justice: Engaging in participatory narrative analysis to find solace in the "killer corridor." *American Journal of Community Psychology*, *55*(1–2), 128–135. https://doi.org/10.1007/s10464-014-9694-7

Drame, E. R., & Irby, D. J. (2016). *Black participatory research: Power, identity, and the struggle for justice in education*. Palgrave.

Du Bois, W. E. B. (1899). *The Philadelphia Negro: A social study*. Ginn.

Du Bois, W. E. B. (2008). *The quest of the silver fleece*. Dover. (Original work published 1911)

Fals Borda, O., & Rahman, M. A. (Eds.). (1991). *Action and knowledge: Breaking the monopoly with participatory action-research*. The Apex Press. https://doi.org/10.3362/9781780444239

Fanon, F. (1952). *Black skin, white masks*. Grove.

Fine, M. (2017). *Just research in contentious times: Expanding the methodological imagination*. Teachers College Press.

Fine, M., & Ruglis, J. (2009). Circuits of dispossession. *Transforming Anthropology, 17*(1), 20–33. https://doi.org/10.1111/j.1548-7466.2009.01037.x

Fine, M., Torre, M. E., Bloom, J., Chajet, L., & Roberts, R. (2004). *Echoes of Brown: Youth documenting and performing the legacy of* Brown v. Board of Education. Teachers College Press.

Fine, M., Torre, M. E., Boudin, K., Bowen, I., Clark, J., Hylton, D., Martinez, M., "Missy," Roberts, R. A., Smart, P., & Upegui, D. (2001). *Changing minds: The impact of college in a maximum-security prison*. https://www.prisonpolicy.org/scans/changing_minds.pdf

Fine, M., Torre, M. E., Boudin, K., Bowen, I., Clark, J., Hylton, D., Martinez, M., "Missy," Roberts, R. A., Smart, P., & Upegui, D. (2003). Participatory action research: From within and beyond prison bars. In P. M. Camic, J. E. Rhodes, & L. Yardley (Eds.), *Qualitative research in psychology: Expanding perspectives in methodology and design* (pp. 173–198). American Psychological Association. https://doi.org/10.1037/10595-010

Fine, M., Torre, M. E., Boudin, K., & Wilkins, C. (2021). Participation, power, and solidarities behind bars: A 25-year reflection on critical participatory action research on college in prison. In P. M. Camic (Ed.), *Qualitative research in psychology: Expanding perspectives in methodology and design* (2nd ed., pp. 85–100). American Psychological Association. https://doi.org/10.1037/0000252-005

Fine, M., Torre, M. E., Frost, D. M., & Cabana, A. L. (2018a). Queer solidarities: New activisms erupting at the intersection of structural precarity and radical misrecognition. *Journal of Social and Political Psychology, 6*(2), 608–630. https://doi.org/10.5964/jspp.v6i2.905

Fine, M., Torre, M. E., Frost, D. M., & Cabana, A. L. (2018b). "Radical by necessity, not by choice": From microaggressions to social activism. In G. C. Torino, D. P. Rivera, C. M. Capodilupo, K. L. Nadal, & D. W. Sue (Eds.), *Microaggression theory: Influence and Implications* (pp. 244–259). Wiley.

Fine, M., Torre, M. E., Frost, D., Cabana, A., & Avory, S. (2018). Refusing to check the box: Participatory inquiry at the radical rim. In K. Gallagher (Ed.), *Methodological dilemmas revisited* (pp. 11–31). Routledge. https://doi.org/10.4324/9781315149325-2

Fine, M., Torre, M., Oswald, A., & Avory, S. (in press). Critical participatory action research: Methods and praxis for intersectional knowledge production. *Journal of Counseling Psychology*.

Fox, M. (2015). Embodied methodologies, participation, and the art of research. *Social and Personality Psychology Compass, 9*(7), 321–332. https://doi.org/10.1111/spc3.12182

Fox, M. (2019). Crossing under the highway: Youth-centered research as resistance to structural inequality. *International Journal of Qualitative Studies in Education, 32*(4), 347–361. https://doi.org/10.1080/09518398.2018.1548042

Freire, P. (1970). *Pedagogy of the oppressed*. Herder & Herder.

Frost, D. M., Fine, M., Torre, M. E., & Cabana, A. (2019). Minority stress, activism, and health in the context of economic precarity: Results from a national participatory action survey of lesbian, gay, bisexual, transgender, queer, and gender non-conforming youth. *American Journal of Community Psychology, 63*(3–4), 511–526. https://doi.org/10.1002/ajcp.12326

Futch, V. A., & Fine, M. (2014). Mapping as a method: History and theoretical commitments. *Qualitative Research in Psychology, 11*(1), 42–59. https://doi.org/10.1080/14780887.2012.719070

Galletta, A. (2013). *Mastering the semi-structured interview and beyond: From research design to analysis and publication*. NYU Press. https://doi.org/10.18574/nyu/9780814732939.001.0001

Galvão, K. (2015). Feminist theory and social justice. *Psicologia e Sociedade, 27*(3), 479–486.

Giraldo-García, R., & Galletta, A. (2015). What happened to our sense of justice? Tracing agency, inquiry, and action in a youth participatory action research (PAR) project. *Journal of Urban Learning, Teaching, and Research, 11*, 91–98.

Greene, M. (1977). Toward wide-awakeness: An argument for the arts and humanities in education. *Teachers College Record, 79*(1), 119–125.

Green Haven Think Tank. (1997). *The non-traditional approach to criminal and social justice*. Center for NuLeadership, Resurrection Study Group.

Guishard, M. (2009). The false paths, the endless labors, the turns now this way and now that: Participatory action research, mutual vulnerability, and the politics of inquiry. *The Urban Review, 41*(1), 85–105. https://doi.org/10.1007/s11256-008-0096-8

Guishard, M., Halkovic, A., Galletta, A., & Li, P. (2018). Toward epistemological ethics: Centering communities and social justice in qualitative research. *Forum Qualitative Social Research, 19*(3). https://doi.org/10.17169/fqs-19.3.3145

Halkovic, A., & Greene, A. C. (2015). Bearing stigma, carrying gifts: What colleges can learn from students with incarceration experience. *The Urban Review, 47*, 759–782. https://doi.org/10.1007/s11256-015-0333-x

Hall, B. (2005). In from the cold? Reflections on participatory research 1970–2005. *Convergence, 38*(1), 5–24.

Harding, S. (1991). *Whose science/whose knowledge? Thinking from women's lives*. Open University Press.

hooks, b. (1984). *Feminist theory: From margin to center*. Routledge.

Horton, M., Kohl, J., & Kohl, H. (1997). *The long haul: An autobiography*. Teachers College Press.

Jahoda, M., Lazarsfeld, P., & Zeisel, H. (2001). *Marienthal: The sociography of an unemployed community*. Transaction.

jones, v., Stewart, C., Ayala, J., & Galletta, A. (2015). Expressions of agency: Contemplating youth voice and adult roles in participatory action research. In J. O. Conner, R. Ebby-Rosin, & A. Slattery (Eds.), *Student voice in American education policy*. Teachers College Press.

Kapoor, D., & Jordan, S. (2019). *Research, political engagement and dispossession: Indigenous, peasant and urban poor activisms in the Americas and Asia*. Zed.

Kirshner, B., & Pozzoboni, K. M. (2011). Student interpretations of a school closure: Implications for student voice in equity-based school reform. *Teachers College Record, 113*(8), 1633–1667.

Lac, V., & Fine, M. (2018). The good, the bad and the ugly: An autoethnographic journey on doing participatory action research as a graduate student. *Urban Education, 53*(4), 562–583. https://doi.org/10.1177/0042085918762491

Land, C. (2015). *Decolonizing solidarity: Dilemmas and directions for supporters of Indigenous struggles*. Zed.

Langhout, R. D., & Vaccarino-Ruiz, S. S. (2020). "Did I see what I really saw?" Violence, percepticide, and dangerous seeing after an Immigration and Customs Enforcement raid. *Journal of Community Psychology*. Advance online publication. https://doi.org/10.1002/jcop.22336

Lee, D. J. (2018). *Delivering justice: Food delivery cyclists in New York City* [Unpublished doctoral dissertation]. The Graduate Center, City University of New York.

Levitt, H. M. (2021). *Essentials of critical-constructivist grounded theory research*. American Psychological Association.

Levitt, H. M., Bamberg, M., Creswell, J. W., Frost, D. M., Josselson, R., & Suárez-Orozco, C. (2017). Journal article reporting standards for qualitative primary, qualitative meta-analytic, and mixed methods research in psychology: The APA Publications and Communications Board Task Force Report. *American Psychologist, 73*(1), 26–46. https://doi.org/10.1037/amp0000151

Lewin, K. (1951). *Field theory in social science*. Harper.

Lorde, A. (1984). *Sister outsider*. Ten Speed Press.

Lugones, M. (2010). Toward a decolonial feminism. *Hypatia, 25*(4), 742–759. https://doi.org/10.1111/j.1527-2001.2010.01137.x

Luttrell, W. (2020). *Children framing childhoods: Working-class kids' visions of care*. University of Chicago Press. https://doi.org/10.2307/j.ctvwcjh0q

Lydon, J., Carrington, K., Low, H., Miller, R., & Yazdy, M. (2015). *Coming out of concrete closets: A report on Black & Pink's National LGBTQ Prisoner Survey*. https://www.issuelab.org/resources/23129/23129.pdf

Maguire, P. (1987). *Doing participatory research: A feminist approach*. University of Massachusetts Scholarworks.

Martín-Baró, I. (1994). *Writings for a liberation psychology*. Harvard University Press.

Massey, S. G., & Barreras, R. E. (2013). Impact validity as a framework for advocacy based research. *Journal of Social Issues, 69*(4), 615–632. https://doi.org/10.1111/josi.12032

McClelland, S. I., & Fine, M. (2008). Writing on cellophane: Studying teen women's sexual desires, inventing methodological release points. In K. Gallagher (Ed.), *The methodological dilemma: Creative, critical, and collaborative approaches to qualitative research* (pp. 232–260). Routledge.

McNulty, J. (2019). Regina Langhout honored for advocacy on behalf of those at risk of deportation. *UC Santa Cruz Newscenter.* https://news.ucsc.edu/2019/04/langhout-award.html

Mills, C. (2012). White ignorance. In S. Sullivan & N. Tuana (Eds.), *Race and epistemologies of ignorance* (pp. 13–38). SUNY Press.

Montgomery, N., & bergman, c. (2017). *Joyful militancy: Building thriving resistance in toxic times.* AK Press.

Morris, A. (2018). American Negro at Paris, 1900. In W. Battle-Baptiste & B. Rusert (Eds.), *W. E. B. Du Bois's data portraits: Visualizing Black America* (pp. 37–51). Princeton Architectural Press.

Munoz-Proto, C. (2009). *Memoscopio.* https://www.memoscopio.org/

Oswald, A., Avory, S., & Fine, M. (in press). Intersectional expansiveness borne at the neuroqueer nexus. *Psychology and Sexuality.*

Payne, Y. (2013). *The people's report.* http://www.thepeoplesreport.com

Pratt, M. L. (1991). Arts of the contact zone. *Profession,* 33–40.

Quan, H. L. T. (Ed.). (2019). *Cedric J. Robinson: On racial capitalism, Black internationalism, and cultures of resistance.* Pluto. https://doi.org/10.2307/j.ctvr0qs8p

Rahman, A. (1985). Theory and practice of participatory action research. In O. Fals Borda (Ed.), *The challenge of social change* (pp. 107–132). SAGE.

Roy, A. (2020, April 3). The pandemic is a portal. *Financial Times.* https://www.ft.com/content/10d8f5e8-74eb-11ea-95fe-fcd274e920ca

Rubin, B. C., Ayala, J., & Zaal, M. (2017). Authenticity, aims and authority: Navigating youth participatory action research in the classroom. *Curriculum Inquiry, 47*(2), 175–194. https://doi.org/10.1080/03626784.2017.1298967

Sandwick, T., Fine, M., Greene, A. C., Stoudt, B. G., Torre, M. E., & Patel, L. (2018). Promise and provocation: Humble reflections on critical participatory action research for social policy. *Urban Education, 53*(4), 473–502. https://doi.org/10.1177/0042085918763513

Sirin, S. R., & Fine, M. (2008). *Muslim American youth: Understanding hyphenated identities through multiple methods.* New York University Press.

Smith, J., Van Deven, M., & Huppuch, M. (2011). *Hey, shorty! A guide to combating sexual harassment and violence in schools and on the streets.* The Feminist Press.

Smith, L. T. (1999). *Decolonizing methodologies: Research and Indigenous people.* Zed.

Stetler, C. (2009). *Junot Diaz: Man in the mirror.* https://www.nj.com/entertainment/arts/2009/10/junot_diaz_man_in_the_mirror.html

Stoudt, B. (2014). Critical statistics. In T. Teo (Ed.), *Encyclopedia of critical psychology* (pp. 1850–1858). Springer. https://doi.org/10.1007/978-1-4614-5583-7_661

Stoudt, B. G. (2016). Conversations on the margins: Using data entry to explore the qualitative potential of survey marginalia. *Qualitative Psychology, 3*(2), 186–208. https://doi.org/10.1037/qup0000060

Stoudt, B. G., Fine, M., & Fox, M. (2011). Growing up policed in the age of aggressive policing policies. *New York Law School Law Review, 56*, 1331–1370.

Stoudt, B. G., Torre, M. E., Bartley, P., Bracy, F., Caldwell, H., Downs, A., Greene, C., Haldipur, J., Hassan, P., Manoff, E., Sheppard, N., & Yates, J. (2016). Participatory action research and policy change. In C. Durose & L. Richardson (Eds.), *Designing public policy for co-production: Theory, practice and change* (pp. 125–137). Policy Press.

Su, C. (2017). Beyond inclusion: Critical race theory and participatory budgeting. *New Political Science, 39*(1), 126–142. https://doi.org/10.1080/07393148. 2017.1278858

Tejawi, A., Halkovic, A., Greene, A., Gary, C., Evans, D., Bae, J., Campbell, L., Ramirez, M., Taylor, M., Fine, M., Tebout, R., & Riggs, R. (2013). *Higher education and re-entry: The gifts they bring.* https://www.issuelab.org/resource/ higher-education-and-reentry-the-gifts-they-bring.html

Teo, T. (2010). What is epistemological violence in the empirical social sciences? *Social and Personality Psychology Compass, 4*(5), 295–303. https://doi.org/ 10.1111/j.1751-9004.2010.00265.x

Torre, M. E. (2009). Participatory action research and critical race theory: Fueling spaces for *nos-otras* to research. *The Urban Review, 41*(1), 106–120. https:// doi.org/10.1007/s11256-008-0097-7

Torre, M. E., Fine, M., Cabana, A., Frost, D., Avery, S., Fowler-Chapman, T., & the What's Your Issue? Youth Research Collective. (2018). Radical wills (and won'ts): Critical participatory inqueery. In S. Talburt (Ed.), *Youth sexualities: Public feelings and contemporary cultural politics* (Vol. 2, pp. 169–191). Praeger.

Torre, M. E., & Fox, M. (2020). *Patterns in the forest: Making connections with inquiry trees.* The Public Science Project Press.

Tuck, E., & Yang, W. (2012). Indigeneity is not a metaphor. *Decolonization, 1*(1), 1–40.

Udvarhelyi, E., & Dosa, M. (2019). *A kutatas felszabadito ereje* [The liberating power of research]. Solar Kiado-Kozelet School.

Vizenor, G. (1999). *Manifest manners: Narratives on postindian survivance.* University of Nebraska Press.

Weis, L., & Fine, M. (2012). Critical bifocality and circuits of privilege. *Harvard Educational Review, 82*(2), 173–201. https://doi.org/10.17763/haer.82.2. v1jx34n441532242

Winnicott, D. W. (1973). *The child, the family, and the outside world.* Penguin.

Zeller-Berkman, S. (2014). Lineages: A past, present and future of participatory action research. In P. Leavy (Ed.), *The Oxford handbook of qualitative research* (pp. 518–531). Oxford University Press.

Zeller-Berkman, S., Barreto, J., & Sandler, A. (2020). Amplifying action: Theories, questions, doubts and hopes related to the "action" phase of a critical participatory action project. *Harvard Educational Review, 90*(2), 229–242. https://doi.org/10.17763/1943-5045-90.2.229

Index

About the Authors

Michelle Fine, PhD, is a Distinguished Professor of Critical Psychology, Women's Studies, Social Welfare, American Studies, and Urban Education at the Graduate Center, City University of New York (CUNY), and founding faculty member of The Public Science Project, a university–community research space designed in collaboration with movements for racial and educational justice. As a scholar, an expert witness in litigation, a teacher, and an educational activist, her work centers theoretically and epistemically on questions of justice and dignity, privilege and oppression, and how solidarities emerge.

Dr. Fine taught at the University of Pennsylvania from 1981 to 1991 and then at the Graduate Center, CUNY. She has served as an expert witness in a range of educational, racial, and gender justice class action lawsuits, including girls suing for access to Central High School in Philadelphia and The Citadel in South Carolina; students of color suing for racial equity in Wedowee, Alabama; youth fighting for equitable financing and facilities in *Williams v. State of California*; and most recently, a finance inequity lawsuit for the children of Baltimore.

With a rich international network of collaborators and activist–scholar colleagues, Dr. Fine has spent time teaching and researching at the Institute for Maori Studies at the University of Auckland in Auckland, New Zealand; the Centre for Narrative Research at the University of East London; the University of Witwatersrand in Johannesburg, South Africa; Universidade Federal de Pernambuco, Brazil; and EuroClio in Nicosia, Cyprus.

Across 30 years, Dr. Fine's key publications include many "classics": books and articles on high school pushouts, adolescent sexuality (called the "missing discourse of desire"), the national evaluation of the impact of college in prison, the struggles and strengths of the children of incarcerated adults, and the wisdom of Muslim American youth, as well as chapters and books on epistemic justice and critical participatory inquiry.

Dr. Fine is the author or coauthor, editor or coeditor, of more than 20 books, including *Just Research in Contentious Times: Expanding the Methodological Imagination* (2017); *Charter Schools and the Corporate Makeover of Public Education: What's at Stake?* (2012); *Muslim American Youth: Understanding Hyphenated Identities Through Multiple Methods* (2008); *Echoes of* Brown: *Youth Documenting and Performing the Legacy of* Brown v. Board of Education (2004); *Changing Minds: The Impact of College in a Maximum-Security Prison* (2001); and *Off White: Readings on Power, Privilege, and Resistance* (2004), among others.

Dr. Fine has been honored with a range of professional awards, including honorary degrees from Bank Street College of Education, Lewis & Clark, and Stanford University and the Distinguished Alumni Award from Teachers College, Columbia University, as well as lifetime achievement awards from the American Psychological Association and the American Educational Research Association.

María Elena Torre, PhD, is the founding director of The Public Science Project. She earned her doctorate at The Graduate Center of the City University of New York, where she is now on the faculty in Critical Social Psychology and Urban Education. Before returning to The Graduate Center, she taught and was chair of Education Studies at Eugene Lang College of Liberal Arts at The New School.

A queer mama of a very cool soon-to-be teenager, she has written about and been engaged in critical participatory action research nationally and internationally for over 20 years, collaborating with communities in neighborhoods, schools, prisons, and community-based organizations seeking social transformation and structural change. With the Public Science Project, Dr. Torre leads annual summer Critical Participatory Action Research (CPAR) Institutes that bring graduate students, faculty, and community workers together to learn alongside each other about the history, theory, methods, and ethics of CPAR. She also facilitates CPAR with government agencies as a way to integrate meaningful community participation and leadership and spark transitions from providing services to supporting community self-determination.

Dr. Torre is an author and editor of *Echoes of* Brown: *Youth Documenting and Performing the Legacy of* Brown v. Board of Education and *PAR EntreMundos: A Pedagogy of the Americas* and has written extensively about how decolonizing methodologies, radical inclusion, and praxis of solidarity can inform a participatory public science that supports movements for justice. She is a recipient the American Psychological Association Division 35 (Society for the Psychology of Women) Adolescent Girls Task Force Emerging Scientist Award, the Spencer Fellowship in Social Justice & Social Development in Educational Studies, and the Michele Alexander Early Career Award for Scholarship and Service from the Society for the Psychological Study of Social Issues of the American Psychological Association. She serves on the editorial boards of *Awry: Journal of Critical Psychology* and the *Review of General Psychology*.

About the Series Editors

Clara E. Hill, PhD, earned her doctorate at Southern Illinois University in 1974. She started her career in 1974 as an assistant professor in the Department of Psychology, University of Maryland, College Park, and is currently there as a professor.

She is the president-elect of the Society for the Advancement of Psychotherapy, and has been the president of the Society for Psychotherapy Research, the editor of the *Journal of Counseling Psychology*, and the editor of *Psychotherapy Research*.

Dr. Hill was awarded the Leona Tyler Award for Lifetime Achievement in Counseling Psychology from Division 17 (Society of Counseling Psychology) and the Distinguished Psychologist Award from Division 29 (Society for the Advancement of Psychotherapy) of the American Psychological Association, the Distinguished Research Career Award from the Society for Psychotherapy Research, and the Outstanding Lifetime Achievement Award from the Section on Counseling and Psychotherapy Process and Outcome Research of the Society of Counseling Psychology. Her major research interests are helping skills, psychotherapy process and outcome, training therapists, dream work, and qualitative research.

She has published more than 250 journal articles, 80 chapters in books, and 17 books (including *Therapist Techniques and Client Outcomes: Eight Cases of Brief Psychotherapy*; *Helping Skills: Facilitating Exploration, Insight, and Action*; and *Dream Work in Therapy: Facilitating Exploration, Insight, and Action*).

Sarah Knox, PhD, joined the faculty of Marquette University in 1999 and is a professor in the Department of Counselor Education and Counseling Psychology in the College of Education. She earned her doctorate at the

University of Maryland and completed her predoctoral internship at The Ohio State University.

Dr. Knox's research has been published in a number of journals, including *The Counseling Psychologist, Counselling Psychology Quarterly, Journal of Counseling Psychology, Psychotherapy, Psychotherapy Research,* and *Training and Education in Professional Psychology.* Her publications focus on the psychotherapy process and relationship, supervision and training, and qualitative research. She has presented her research both nationally and internationally and has provided workshops on consensual qualitative research at both U.S. and international venues.

She currently serves as coeditor-in-chief of *Counselling Psychology Quarterly* and is also on the publication board of Division 29 (Society for the Advancement of Psychotherapy) of the American Psychological Association. Dr. Knox is a fellow of Division 17 (Society of Counseling Psychology) and Division 29 of the American Psychological Association.